CHAUCER AND THE FRENCH LOVE POETS

UNIVERSITY OF NORTH CAROLINA
STUDIES IN COMPARATIVE LITERATURE

Founded by Werner P. Friederich

Editorial Committee

William J. DeSua, Editor

For Reprints from this Series see page 185.

Foreign Sales through Librairie E. Droz, 11 Rue Massot, Geneva, Switzerland.

CHAUCER AND THE FRENCH LOVE POETS

THE LITERARY BACKGROUND OF THE
BOOK OF THE DUCHESS

by

JAMES WIMSATT

CHAPEL HILL
THE UNIVERSITY OF NORTH CAROLINA PRESS
1968

Printed in the Netherlands by Royal VanGorcum Ltd., Assen

FOR MARY ANN

ACKNOWLEDGMENTS

In the development of this book many individuals have provided assistance and encouragement. Among these I wish to mention particularly Holger O. Nygard, Robert E. Kaske, Robert M. Lumiansky, Joseph A. Bryant, Jr., Urban T. Holmes, Jr., and (most particularly) my wife, Mary Ann. I am grateful also to the editors of the University of North Carolina Series in Comparative Literature for their helpful suggestions. I have had personal financial assistance from Duke University, the Southern Fellowships Fund, and the Southeastern Institute of Medieval and Renaissance Studies. The typing and publication of this study have been aided by grants from the Research Committee of the University of North Carolina at Greensboro.

CONTENTS

INTRODUCTION

Because the development of the French love narrative after Guillaume de Lorris' *Roman de la Rose* (c. 1230) through the fifteenth century is a story that few have found interesting, it has remained virtually untold. Perhaps its outlines after Guillaume de Machaut's love poems (i.e., after c. 1365) are fairly clear, for the important writers of this later period—Froissart, Deschamps, Christine de Pisan, and Alain Chartier—all continued modes substantially originated or refined by Machaut. But the progress of the love narrative up to Machaut is more complicated and has been left unillumined; even the works of Machaut himself have evoked a minimum of scholarly interest, less than the poetry of such of his disciples as Jean Froissart and Christine de Pisan.

Yet for the Chaucerian scholar the story is worth telling. Chaucer's first long poem, the *Book of the Duchess*, with which the great bulk of his later work has significant affinity, is squarely in the line of development of the French love narrative and is particularly indebted to Machaut's works in both form and content. Chaucer to be sure carries one great step further the evolution which took place between the *Roman de la Rose* and Machaut's work, but the parentage of the poem is unmistakable. In this study, then, I propose to show how the French love narrative evolved from Guillaume de Lorris to the time of the *Book of the Duchess* (1369), and then to inspect the immediate relationship between the *Duchess* and its contemporary sources. These

1

sources have been mostly enumerated, but the general nature of their relationships to each other and to Chaucer's poem has not been established.

The stages by which the *dit amoreux* (a convenient name for the French love narrative) became what it was in 1369 are not sharply defined, though there is assuredly a progressive development. One factor which blurs the picture is the continuing importance of the *Roman de la Rose* as a primary source. It is often difficult to determine whether its influence is direct or indirect, since it cannot be doubted that every writer with whom this study is concerned was familiar with the *Roman de la Rose* and made use of it. This is emphatically true of Chaucer, who translated the poem. Thus in the first chapter it has been thought appropriate to deal at some length with Guillaume's *Roman de la Rose* and the *Book of the Duchess*, not only to establish the point at which the study begins and to inspect the poem of Chaucer which will be primarily in question throughout but also to make clear from the outset what elements of the *Duchess* can be ascribed to the immediate influence of Guillaume de Lorris.

In the next two chapters, *dits amoreux* which were written between Guillaume de Lorris' poem and the poems of Guillaume de Machaut are classified and discussed, and certain tendencies in the development of this genre are identified. Consideration of the works of Machaut occupies the three chapters which then follow. In these Machaut's poetry is surveyed and several of his *dits* which were especially influential on Chaucer are inspected rather closely, including the two debate poems and the two narratives of "complaint and comfort." Two chapters dealing with poems of complaint and comfort of other authors, in which it is suggested that some works of this type have been thought of erroneously as sources for the *Duchess*, conclude the study.

Charles Muscatine begins his admirable *Chaucer and the French Tradition* by noting that critical studies such as his go beyond "post-Victorian" work. "Liberated in great measure by post-Victorian scholarship itself," he says, his own criticism "does not confine itself to narrowly textual sources in tracing and using the literary history behind Chaucer."[1] My work is, I fear, mostly unliberated. But it is designed to liberate by providing subsequent critics a coherent picture of material which has not been previously the subject of a single treatment. No history of French literature has dealt in a remotely comprehensive fashion with the poems considered in this study; no monograph has analyzed and evaluated Machaut's literary career; and no attempt has been made to show the interrelationships of the sources of the *Book of the Duchess*. Only two previous critical studies, now very old, have even dealt with a substantial number of the works taken up here: William A. Neilson's *Origins and Sources of the Court of Love*[2] and Wilbur O. Sypherd's *Studies in Chaucer's House of Fame*.[3] These merely afford fragmentary descriptions of several of the individual works.

I have attempted to supply the lack on all sides in some fashion. In addition to tracing out the development of the *dits amoreux*, I have furnished historical material about the authors and works, and have referred to articles and books about them; I have thought it desirable to sketch out Machaut's poetic achievement; and I have not hesitated to round out the summaries of the poems with details which are not strictly relevant to the whole development. The process of incorporating this material into one short book perhaps has led, despite my efforts, to some tediousness. The many summaries, for instance, must assume a sameness to the reader who goes through this book at one sitting. But I have thought it expedient rather to include relevant material than to exclude it simply to make the reading easier. If this book accomplishes its purpose it will help others to make the kind of liberated observations which comprise Professor Muscatine's book. Had such a work as this existed when he was writing, perhaps he himself would have been led to devote more than three pages to the French love poems which intervene between Guillaume de Lorris and Chaucer.

The Appendix provided here charts Chaucer's line-for-line

borrowings and possible borrowings for the *Duchess*. In great part it is compiled from the source studies of Kittredge[4] and from editors' notes. It also includes identifications and suggestions of line sources which I make herein and elsewhere. The information supplied in the Appendix thus supplements the more general consideration of the literary background which is the main preoccupation of this work.

CHAPTER I

GUILLAUME DE LORRIS AND
THE *BOOK OF THE DUCHESS*

The *Roman de la Rose* was the last great manifestation of the twelfth- and thirteenth-century flowering of French poetry, when important epics, romances, lays, and lyrics proliferated. The reputation of this poem today is in no way comparable to that which it enjoyed in its own time. The number of surviving manuscripts is an eloquent witness to its popularity, for, whereas the 84 extant manuscripts of the *Canterbury Tales* testify to an extraordinary currency for that work, more than 300 manuscripts remain of the poem of Guillaume de Lorris and Jean de Meun. And its tremendous prestige extended beyond the reading public to the writers, so that it is difficult to name a French or English poet of the two centuries following its composition whose writings do not bear the strong imprint of the *Roman de la Rose*.

The pervasiveness of its influence results in part from the fact that the *Rose* is two poems: an idealized courtly poem by Guillaume, and a realistic bourgeois poem by Jean.[1] Because of this it could, and did, leave its stamp on both courtly and realistic literature. Thus Chaucer, the most famous evangelist of the *Roman de la Rose*, reflects the work in his lyric and vision poetry on the one hand, and in characterizations like the Wife of Bath and Pandarus on the other. In the *Book of the Duchess*, and in the French poems which are to be taken up in this study, the indebtedness to the *Rose* is chiefly to Guillaume's 4058-line section. The analysis and summary which follow, therefore, are limited to that part.

5

For Guillaume's narrative I posit three major divisions. The story begins with fourteen hundred lines of prefatory narrative and description, which lead to the lover's first contact with his lady at the pool of Narcissus. The next thirteen hundred lines are a mixed allegory involving this pool, the rose garden, the God of Love's personified artillery, and a lecture by the God of Love devoted mostly to the practical aspects of love. Only in the final thirteen hundred lines does the allegory become centered on the rose garden, though even here the allegorical cadre is developed without scrupulous regard to consistency.[2]

In the forty-four lines which precede the dream, the poet calls Macrobius to witness that some dreams come true, and states that he had a true dream in his twentieth year, with nothing in it which did not subsequently happen. The story, which he promises to relate now in rhyme, is called the Romance of the Rose and has an Art of Love enclosed in it. The poet asks God to grant that she for whom he makes the poem receive it willingly.

The narrator then tells about waking up in his dream in Maytime. Having dressed, he walks along the bank of a clear, fresh river—in which he washes his face—till he comes to an enclosed garden, on the walls of which are painted various personified figures whose appearance he describes in detail (ll. 139-462): Haine, Felonie, Vilanie, Covoitise, Avarice, Envie, Tristece, Vieillece, Papelardie, and Povreté. These descriptions of abstractions found outside—excluded from—the garden begin the process of definition of this garden and its activities. Not only such conventional sins as Covetousness, Avarice, Envy, and Hate, but also such natural defects as Old Age, Poverty, and Sadness, are excluded.

The singing of birds inside the garden makes the dreamer long to enter; his anxious search for a gate reveals a small closed wicket, on which he knocks persistently until it is opened by Oiseuse, who is a courtly beauty. The dreamer's entry into the garden symbolizes his entry into a new life. But before he embarks on his new career, he finds out what the garden is like.

6

Since Oiseuse has charge of the door, the garden is obviously a place to relax; she herself has nothing to do but play and comb her hair. She is a good friend of Deduit, who owns the garden, from which one may further infer that the garden above all provides delight. At the dreamer's request, Oiseuse leads him to Deduit; the dreamer enumerates the many beautiful birds they see on the way. Deduit and his company are dancing in a *carole*, and many minstrels, jugglers, and other entertainers are performing. Cortoisie invites the dreamer to dance with the group, and he joins them. He describes each of the carolers (ll. 801-1278), these descriptions balancing those of the unhappy group outside and contributing further to the definition of the garden. Deduit is accompanied by Leece; the God of Love is with Douz Regarz, his bow-and-arrow carrier, and with Biautez; Richese has an unnamed escort; Largece has a knight of King Arthur (probably Lancelot); Jonece knows no better than to kiss her lover right out in the open; and finally Franchise and Cortoisie are with handsome *bachelers*.

As the reader is learning about the garden so also is the dreamer being instructed by what he sees in preparation for his love experience, which is about to begin when he leaves the carole (l. 1279). While Amor follows him with his bow drawn, the dreamer wanders around the garden which is filled with trees of different species. Deer and rabbits abound, and many flowers freckle the garden with their color. Finally, under a great pine he finds the fountain where Narcissus died, and he tells the story of Narcissus at some length. Then the dreamer looks down into the spring at the clear water and the two rocks of crystal on the bottom, which evidently represent the eyes of a lady.[3] These crystals have wonderful power in love; they reflect the whole garden, and in this reflection a group of rose bushes arrests the dreamer's gaze. He approaches the rose arbor, and among the roses one bud of singular perfection catches his eye. He would take it, but the briars and thorns impede him.

The nature of the pool, that in which Narcissus died for love of himself, seems further to define the kind of love found in the Garden of Deduit. It assuredly bodes no good for the dreamer. The transition from the pool to the rose bushes is skillfully handled, with the bushes which the dreamer approaches being reflected in the crystals of the pool; it almost escapes the reader's notice that the vehicles of the allegory have been radically switched. Instead of in the crystals, the lady's attractiveness is now embodied in the Rose. Another radical change, which is more apparent, takes place just after the dreamer has found himself unable to claim his chosen rosebud. At this point (l. 1681) Amor, who has been following all the time, shoots him with five arrows: Biauté, Simplece, Cortoisie, Compaignie, and Biau Semblant. If it were not for the soothing ointment which Amor put on the last arrow (Biau Semblant, the encouraging look), the dreamer claims that he would have died right there, a martyr to Love. But the God of Love wishes to have him as a vassal, and he approaches the dreamer and demands that he become his liege, to which the dreamer—in no condition to refuse—readily assents. Amor locks up the dreamer's heart for security against misbehavior, and then delivers a long sermon on the proper practices of a lover.

This sermon (ll. 2023-2765) may be the "Art of Love" to which Guillaume refers at the beginning of the poem. Certainly it consists of the type of instruction which Ovid includes in his treatise. (At the same time, the whole of the *Roman de la Rose* may be seen as a manual for lovers.) Amor says first that the *amant* should avoid vulgarity, slander, and filthy language, should honor and serve all ladies, and do things to please them so that he will be spoken of well. He should dress as well as he can afford, keep his hands and teeth clean, and his hair combed, but he should not paint his face. He should be gay and show off his skills, whether in riding, jousting, dancing, or fluting; and he should be generous.

Amor then warns of experiences to come, the pains and consolations of love. The lover always longs to see his lady, Amor

8

states, and he seeks her out; but finding her only feeds the fire. When talking to her he is hardly able to speak, and he forgets what he has wanted to say. At night he lies in bed imagining that he has his lady naked in his arms; then, coming to himself, he wishes he had died in the bliss of his imagination. He lies waiting for morning and gets up before dawn in hail or sleet to walk to the lady's house. When he gets there, Amor advises, he should let his lady know his love by sighing loudly through an open window or through the keyhole. Amor in conclusion promises that he will be consoled in his distress by certain of Amor's agents: Esperance, which even a robber about to hang has; Douz Parlers, particularly the sweet words spoken by a trusted friend who praises the lady's virtues; Douz Regarz, denied to those far away from their loved ones; and Douz Pensers, memory of her sweetness. Later, says Amor, he will have other greater goods, but for the time these must suffice. Amor vanishes after this discourse, leaving little doubt with the reader that the love in question is one in which practical means are used to secure physical possession of the beloved. The means and the object are quite like those in Ovid's *Art of Love*, though Guillaume's treatise lacks the cynicism towards women of Ovid's work.

Amor gone, the allegory once more centers on the rose garden, which is the focus for the rest of the work though all of its surroundings undergo a metamorphosis. The dreamer again pondering how to get to his chosen rose, Bel Acueil comes up and leads him right to the bush. Dangier, Malebouche, Honte, and Peor are close by, but they do not cause any trouble till the dreamer outrages Bel Acueil by asking permission to pick the bud. Then, Dangier—big, dark, and unkempt—comes up quickly and irately, and the dreamer has to leave the enclosure. Raison at this point descends from her tower and lectures the dreamer against Amor, advising him to leave such vain service; but the dreamer responds that Raison is wasting her French, that he will always serve Amor faithfully. So Raison leaves.

By this time the whole garden has suffered a sea-change. It is

9

no longer a place where the dreamer walks around admiring sights that consist in great part of personifications unattached to people. Instead it has become a psychological landscape, with the dreamer now involved in an allegory wherein both he and the lady are represented and influenced by personifications and other abstract figures. The lady's part is carried by personified qualities of her personality—Bel Acueil, Dangier, Honte, Franchise, etc.—and by abstractions representing people associated with her—Malebouche, the slanderer; Jalosie, the husband and relatives; and La Vieille, the experienced old maid-servant. Through the abstract character of Amant the dreamer deals with the lady; Raison, his own good sense personified, argues with him; and Ami, the sympathetic friend, encourages him. Neither the tower of Raison nor the castle later built by Jalosie has, of course, any reasonable place in the original Garden of Deduit, which only makes more clear the fact that the ground-rules of the allegorical representation have changed.

After Raison leaves (l. 3096), the dreamer feels desolate till he remembers Amor's advice, whereupon he seeks out Ami, who encourages him to believe that Dangier is not so bad as he looks. The lover returns to the hedge, and Dangier indeed, after some cajolery, does allow him to look at the rose bed from outside the protective hedge; and after a while, as a result of some coercion by Franchise and Pitié, Dangier once more permits the suffering Amant the company of Bel Acueil. He now finds on close inspection that the bud is more open and even more beautiful than before. With the help of Venus, who warms up Bel Acueil with her brand, he is granted a kiss. The perfume from the kiss enters his heart and soothes all the wounds which the arrows of Amor had made. But his joy does not last.

The last five hundred lines (3511-4058) bring Guillaume de Lorris' story to a dramatic close. Malebouche sees the kiss and wakes up Jalosie, who runs up to Bel Acueil, reviling him; the dreamer is once more forced to leave the area. Jalosie rages to Honte and Peor that they are no longer sufficient guards for

10

Bel Acueil. They in turn go and reproach Dangier—who is sleeping pillowed on a mound of turf under a hawthorn tree—for not doing his job; they say that it does not suit his name that he be courteous, that people think him stupid when they see him affable. This enrages Dangier, who picks up his club and stalks around the enclosure, again ready to attack intruders. Jalosie, however, will take no further chances and now hires workmen from all over the country who build a castle with a square wall, a hundred fathoms on a side with a turret at each corner. In the center of the enclosed area a high tower is set in which Bel Acueil is imprisoned. Dangier, Honte, Peor, and Malebouche guard each of the four gates in the wall; and Malebouche takes the watch at night, when he sings from the top of the wall about the faults of women. An old woman, who knows from experience all the "old dance" of love, is put to guard Bel Acueil. The poem ends with the dreamer addressing Bel Acueil rhetorically, telling him not to let Jalosie put his heart in servitude along with his body. And he pleads that Bel Acueil not forget him, for he will never have comfort if he loses Bel Acueil's *bienvoillance*.

Like Chaucer who left several of his works unfinished, Guillaume de Lorris left his romance apparently incomplete; in his own century Jean de Meun (along with an anonymous poet who wrote a 78-line conclusion) took it to be so, as his continuation and conclusion to the poem indicate. One might speculate that Guillaume had no intention of finishing it, though this would involve explaining away the lines in which Guillaume promises to tell how Amor took Jalosie's castle.[4] Nevertheless, when Guillaume's poem ends with the lover addressing a prayer to Bel Acueil, asking him to keep his heart true despite his bodily imprisonment, the story has a certain completeness. It is certainly not incomplete in the same way that Chaucer's Cook's Tale is incomplete.

Aside from the fact that it seems unfinished, however, there are numerous more integral similarities in Guillaume's poem to Chaucer's works, especially to the *Book of the Duchess*. An analysis of the narrative of the *Duchess* will facilitate a comparison of that work to Guillaume's poem.

In the past, disagreement has been expressed with the identification of Chaucer's Black Knight and his mistress as John of Gaunt and his wife, Blanche; such disagreement has very recently been stated again by D. W. Robertson, Jr., as regards the Knight.[5] However, the lady is called *White* (l. 948); and John of Gaunt's titles of *Richmond* and *Lancaster*, along with the Christian names of both husband and wife, are scarcely disguised in the lines toward the end of the poem which describe the castle toward which the Black Knight rides:

> A *long castel* with walles *White*,
> Be seynt *Johan*! on a *ryche hil*...[6]

If a precedent for this kind of identification is needed, one may cite Machaut's custom of identifying the subjects of his poems anagrammatically, as he signifies the Duc de Berry and himself in the very important source of the *Duchess*, the *Dit de la Fonteinne amoreuse*.[7] In any event it is assumed in this study that John and his Duchess are—at least on one level—the poetic subjects. Blanche died in September, 1369, and it seems likely that the poem was written shortly afterward.

The *Book of the Duchess* may be said to have four chief divisions. There is first of all the section which frames the dream, which includes everything before the poet goes to sleep and after he wakes up. The second division is a second frame: within the dream the description of the garden and the hunt frames the elegy. The elegy proper is made up of the other two major sections, the complaints of the knight and his story of his love.

The part of the frame which precedes the dream is taken up with discussion of the narrator's problem in getting to sleep, and includes a long Ovidian exemplum. The poet begins by stating that he cannot sleep day or night. He supposes that his sleeplessness results from the sickness that he has endured for eight years. Only one physician can heal him, he continues (his lady,

12

we must assume), but he wants to pass over that subject for now and deal with "our first mater." The other night, while he was in bed trying to sleep, he read a book in which he found a wonderful tale. The story (ll. 62-220) is about a king named Seys who drowns at sea; his wife, Alcyone, ignorant of what has happened, has him sought for east and west, but in vain. Desperate, she prays to her goddess Juno to send word of her husband. After Alcyone falls into a deep sleep, Juno dispatches her messenger to tell Morpheus to appear as Seys to Alcyone and reveal to her his death. The messenger goes to the cave of Sleep, blows his horn into the sleeping Morpheus' ear, and gives him his orders. After Morpheus shows Alcyone that Seys is drowned, the queen herself dies within three days. But, interrupts the poet, I cannot elaborate on the ending of this story now; I want to tell you how this tale relates to "my first matere." In the next seventy lines (221-290), he tells how after reading the story, he playfully (though he did not feel very playful, he interpolates) offers Morpheus and Juno a number of gifts, including a feather-bed and pillows, if they will help him sleep. Immediately he is over-whelmed by sleep and has a marvellous dream which would almost defy the interpretation of Joseph and Macrobius.

The second frame (ll. 291-442, 1311-24), a frame-within-a-frame, begins within the dream. It leads to the elegy but does not belong to it in any direct sense. In the dream it is May; the narrator is awakened in his bed, it seems to him, by a great gathering of small birds, who are singing outside his chamber the most solemn service that man has ever heard. He notices that the windows of his room are glazed with the story of Troy, and that the walls are painted with both text and gloss of the Romance of the Rose. As he lies there, he hears someone testing a hunting horn and men on horseback talking about a hunt. Straightway he takes his horse and joins the "route," finding that it is Emperor Octavian's party. The hounds are soon uncoupled, a hart is started but gets away, and the signal is blown that the dogs are far off the scent. As the dreamer stands by his tree

13

(evidently his station for the hunt) a puppy comes up; trying to catch the puppy, he follows it into a flowery grove. The tremendous trees there have branches completely shutting out the sun, and there are innumerable bucks, does, and squirrels.

The scene is finally set for the elegy, presented first by means of the lover's complaints, which are initially generalized (ll. 443-616), then are directed specifically against Fortune (ll. 617-720). As the animals roam away from the dreamer, he becomes aware of a knight dressed in black sitting there. This knight, very pale, recites a "maner lay" of eleven lines in which he complains because Death did not take him when it took his lady. When, after almost swooning, he finally notices the dreamer, he gently apologizes for his abstraction. The dreamer asks the knight to tell him his trouble so that he can help him if at all possible. Not even Galen can cure him, the Black Knight replies. Death itself flees him; his health has turned to sickness, his love to hate, his sleeping into waking, and his peace into arguing and war. The Black Knight now singles out Fortune; he says that he has played a game of chess with that hypocrite, traitress, and scorpion, and lost his *fers* (queen). Then he reconsiders (in a Boethian reversal) that Fortune is as she is, and that he would have done the same thing had he been she. Still, he sighs, there is nothing left for him but to die, and soon. The dreamer reminds the knight that Socrates did not care three straws for what Fortune could do, but the knight replies, "I can no soo."

The dreamer's rejoinder at this point leads into the Black Knight's story (ll. 721-1310). Even though he had lost twelve queens, says the dreamer, if he killed himself he would be damned just as surely as Medea, Phyllis, and Dido were damned for killing themselves for love. The knight answers that he has lost more than the dreamer can imagine, and that he will tell the story if the dreamer promises to listen carefully. The knight goes on to say that he chose love as his "first craft" before malice had a chance to mar his nature through his knowing too much. But his "werkes were flyttynge" and his "thoght varyinge" at

14

this time. Then Fortune one day brought him into a company of lovely ladies; among them was one who was more beautiful than the rest in the same way as the sun outshines the moon and stars.

A lengthy description of the lady (ll. 817-1087) now precedes the narration of the love affair. Her hair was perfect gold; her eyes seemed merciful; she had a sweet, soft, eloquent speech. Her throat was like a round tower of ivory, and she was called "goode faire White." She could play so charmingly that she was like the torch that can supply fire to everyone and have no less light itself. She had as much goodness in her as had Esther; Truth himself had made her his chief home. And she did not put off men with promises, nor did she send men on pilgrimages for her to the Dry Sea. He was struck with love for her; she became his hap, health, bliss, and goodness. The dreamer chimes in here to agree that the lady was no doubt quite lovely; but the studied moderation of this statement incites the knight to insist that not only was she beautiful, but also that everyone who saw her agreed that she was the most beautiful. However strong, rich, or handsome he had been himself, he exclaims, he would have had to love her, for she was as good as Penelope or Lucrece.

The Black Knight then tells the events after this first sight of his mistress. As long as he could look at her, she amended all his sorrow. To repent loving her would make him a traitor worse than Achitophel, Antenor, or Ganelon; but now, he adds, he has lost her. The dreamer asks what happened; would the lady not love him, or did he misbehave so that she left him? Working by degrees up to an answer to this question, the knight explains how at first he was unable to profess his love to his lady, for he was afraid of being rebuffed; so he secretly made songs to her (he recites a six-line example of one). Later he summoned up the courage to tell her his love, but she refused to encourage him. After he proved himself by faithful service, however, she granted him mercy, "Savynge her worship." Then they lived in happiness for many years. "Where is she now?" asks the dreamer. "She ys ded!" "Is that youre los? Be God, hyt ys routhe!"

Both frames, the hunt and the dream, are quickly closed (ll. 1311-34). The dreamer says that the hunters all "gan to strake forth," and the knight, now identified as "this king," rides home to his nearby castle. Just then the bell in the castle tower strikes twelve, and the poet is awakened. He finds himself lying in his bed with his book, and he resolves to put the dream into rhyme.

The *Roman de la Rose* is primarily important to the *Book of the Duchess* as the progenitor of the love narratives, *dits amoreux*, from which Chaucer's poem developed. However, its immediate influence on the *Duchess* is also appreciable. The plan of Chaucer's long prologue has its closest analogue in the *Rose*, as I will demonstrate later in this chapter. Furthermore, the *Rose* is the direct source for much of the dream sequence which precedes the elegy (i.e., for the second frame) of Chaucer's poem. In this sequence Chaucer's story runs parallel to the introductory part of the *Rose*: both narrators, having called to witness Macrobius' Dream of Scipio,[8] tell about waking up in bed and taking an eventful walk through the countryside, finally being led through an unobtrusive entrance into an earthly paradise. As the narratives are concurrent here, so also the details of the descriptions of birds, deer, squirrels, and plant life are clearly related.

Chaucer and all of the French poets went back to Guillaume particularly for such details. For them, and even for the modern reader, his garden is magical. His preoccupation with birds throughout the first part of the *Rose* initially helps to convey a sense of paradise. Birds signal the joy of the season when the narrator first notes the beauty of May:

> Li oisel, qui se sont teu
> Tant come il ont le froit eu
> E le tens divers e frarin,
> Sont en mai, por le tens serin,
> Si lié qu'il montrent en chantant
> Qu'en lor cuers a de joie tant
> Qu'il lor estuet chanter par force.
> Li rossigniaus lores s'esforce

16

De chanter e de faire noise;
Lors se deduit e lors s'envoise
Li papegauz e la calandre. (ll. 67-77)

The dreamer says that young people are prompted to love by the
piteus song of the birds (ll. 81-83). He goes on his walk for the
specific purpose of listening to their song (ll. 93-97). As he goes
along he hears them *s'angoissant* to express their bliss (ll. 99-102).
From outside the walled garden he hears singing therein three
times as many birds as populate all France (ll. 478-483). Their
song motivates his desperate desire to enter the garden (ll. 484-
492); they are now explicitly singing the songs of Love:

Les dances d'amors e les notes
Plaisanz, cortoises e mignotes. (ll. 495-496)

Oiseuse, who opens the gate to the Amant, mentions the singing
of the nightingale and thrush among the delights to be found
inside (ll. 609-610). Once inside, the narrator catalogues the
species that are vying to out-sing each other (ll. 643-660),
describes their symphony as a *servise*, and compares them to
angels and then to sirens (ll. 661-674). Wholly delighted by them
(ll. 675-680), he elaborates on the conception of a service, which
he says consists of *lays* of love, courtly *sonets* and *serventois*. The
birds are even singing in harmony, "li un en haut, li autre en bas"
(ll. 701-711). After this, however, Guillaume finds no further
occasion to describe birds except for the popinjays, nightingales,
calendar larks, and titmice embroidered on the God of Love's
coat.

Chaucer's bird description in the *Duchess* is limited to a single
sizeable passage drawn eclectically from the various sequences
just cited of the *Rose*:

Me thoghte thus: that hyt was May,
And in the dawenynge I lay
(Me mette thus) in my bed al naked,
And loked forth, for I was waked
With smale foules a gret hep

17

That had affrayed me out of my slep,
Thorgh noyse and swetnesse of her song.
And, as me mette, they sate among
Upon my chambre roof wythoute,
Upon the tyles, overal aboute,
And songen, everych in hys wyse,
The moste solempne servise
By noote, that ever man, y trowe,
Had herd; for som of hem song lowe,
Som high, and al of oon acord.
To telle shortly, att oo word,
Was never herd so swete a steven,—
But hyt had be a thyng of heven,—
So mery a soun, so swete entewnes,
That certes, for the toun of Tewnes,
I nolde but I had herd hem synge;
For al my chambre gan to rynge
Thurgh syngynge of her armonye.
For instrument nor melodye
Was nowhere herd yet half so swete,
Nor of acord half so mete;
For there was noon of hem that feyned
To synge, for ech of hem hym peyned
To fynde out mery crafty notes.
They ne spared not her throtes.   (ll. 291-320)

In the birds' awakening the narrator, Chaucer's story differs from Guillaume's, whose Amant hears no birds till he gets outside. Chaucer elaborates considerably on the conception of them singing in "armonye," which Guillaume had suggested. The narrator's statement in the *Duchess* that he would not have traded the town of Tunis for their serenade is only analogous to— though quite evidently inspired by—the lover's avowal in the *Rose* that, after hearing the birds from outside the garden, he would not have stopped at paying a hundred *livres* to get inside (ll. 488-490). The remainder of these lines is taken over with little variation from Guillaume.

Almost every other poem in the tradition makes some use of birds. Near the beginning of Machaut's *Dit dou Roy de Behaing-*

18

ne, the narrator relates that he was walking along to the song of birds till one flying above the rest and calling *oci* caught his attention and led him into the woods where he sat down to listen to the singing.[9] The lover in the same poet's *Remede de Fortune* is so engrossed with his problems that he does not notice the birds in the park until after his vision of Esperence, but later he observes them in thirty thousand places, mouths gaping, making the woods ring with their melody (ll. 2981-3008). Machaut consistently devotes a few lines of his *dits* to the birds' song, but generally no more. Froissart is more detailed in his nature description than Machaut; in *Paradys d'Amours* he describes lyrically and at some length the birds' joyful singing.[10]

There are numerous other appearances of birds in the *dits amoreux;* among these is the fifty-line conversation in Watriquet de Couvin's *Tournois des dames* which birds carry on about their happiness in the new season:

> [le douz rossignol]
> Lors renforce son chant et crie:
> "Fier, fier, ochi, ochi, ochi!"
> Li mauvis respont: "Vez le chi
> Oprimes le temps qui m'agrée
> Et la saison plus desirée
> D'amie et de loial ami."[11]

The lover of Thibaut's *Romanz de la Poire* sends his lady a nightingale as a love-token (ll. 2932 ff.); and birds actually carry the narrator of Nicole de Margival's *Panthère d'Amours* into the woods (ll. 47 ff.).[12] In Chaucer's other dream poems, birds of all sorts provide the title episode of the *Parliament of Fowls* (and sing a wonderful *roundel*), and the singing of little birds supplies a number of lyric lines in the *Legend of Good Women* Prologue (especially F, 130-170).

The direct source for the wording in the *Duchess* which describes the *servise* of birds (ll. 301-305) is manifestly the *Roman de la Rose,* but Machaut supplies Chaucer with other precedents. In *Behaingne* the Knight talks about the *beau servise* of birds (ll. 1509-13); birds in the *Jugement dou Roy de Navarre* are said to hold a *chapitre* (i.e., a religious assembly, 1. 8); and with a change in the meaning of *service*, each of the birds in the *Dit dou Lyon* is said to render "loange et servise" to the springtime (ll. 73-74). Before Machaut, Jean de Condé had picked up the idea of a service of birds from the *Roman de la Rose* and developed it to what is surely its fullest potential. In his *Messe des oisiaus et plais des chanonesses et des grises nonains*, Jean devotes more than three hundred lines to describing the Mass, presided over by Venus, which various song-birds take turns in singing from Confiteor to Last Gospel.[13]

Most other details of Chaucer's garden and dream sequence also come ultimately from the *Roman de la Rose*. From the chamber in which the narrator is awakened by the birds Chaucer gracefully moves the locale of his poem outdoors, with the sound of the horn introducing the sequence of the hunt. After the deer is lost, a little dog leads the narrator into a marvellous garden-spot by a seldom-used path:

> And I hym folwed, and hyt forth wente
> Doun by a floury grene wente
> Ful thikke of gras, ful softe and swete,
> With floures fele, faire under fete,
> And litel used, hyt semed thus. (ll. 397-401)

The little path here serves the same function as the small wicket of the *Roman de la Rose*; it is the secret way into the miraculous garden spot. Machaut on occasion utilizes both a gate and a narrow path to lead into his gardens-apart; and in his *Dit dou Lyon* a magic boat is the single possible means of access to the *vergier*. Watriquet makes use of nearly inaccessible gardens in a number of poems, as in the *Dit de l'Arbre royal*, in which he dreams that he is transported to a garden in his sleep:

> Endormi tout a cuer joiant
> En .i. bel vergier verdoiant
> Loing de la ville, en .i. destour

20

Enclos d'un haut mur tout entour
Crestelé de pierre et de marbre... (ll. 19-23)

Destour—a little out-of-the-way spot—is a favorite designation
of the site of the garden in the *dits amoreux*. Often the spot opens
out into a whole world of natural perfection, of supernatural
marvels, and of wonderful abstract beings. This is what happens
in Froissart's *Paradys d'Amours*; from the pleasance which
Amant finds beside the river, Esperance and Plaisance lead him
through all the kingdom of Amor, through the land of the hounds
and huntsmen of Love, past the *carole* of the heroes and martyrs
of Love. The little unused path, the wicket gate, then, are the
ways to wonderland. And wonderland is what the dreamer of
the *Duchess* finds: flowers and animals without number, immense
trees, and a very perfect, though very mournful, knight.

The path, of course, simply helps to bring about another in a
series of removes from the real world which Chaucer effects in the
Duchess. The fact of the dream is the first remove; then the scene
of the poem moves away from the bed where reality is latent,
through the wonderful chamber, into a marvellous countryside
where the legendary Octavian is hunting, and finally down the
"floury grene wente." This process of withdrawal from the world
of fact into the world of the vision is quite analogous to the
process employed by Guillaume de Lorris. In the *Rose* the
dreamer goes from his chamber to the river, into the garden, and
at length to the rose arbor.

The garden-spot into which the puppy leads Chaucer's dreamer
is filled with flowers thick underfoot, trees towering overhead,
and innumerable animals, which are all described in terms that
Guillaume uses (except for a part of the flower description
[ll. 402-409] which comes from Jean's section of the *Rose*). In
the forty-three lines of Chaucer's description (ll. 400-442), there is
a source in the *Rose* for all lines except the first two.[14] Chaucer
went directly to Guillaume's poem for this description not only
because it provides a classic description of a *locus amoenus*, but

21

also because it provides by far the fullest description of a garden to be found among the *dits amoreux* which preceded the *Duchess*.[15] It is not that the later poets found the garden unimportant; on the contrary, it is the garden-apart rather than the dream which is the most pervasive feature of these poems. It rather seems that Guillaume de Lorris' successors felt that a partial or sketchy depiction of the garden of the *Rose* was sufficient to evoke that magical locale. Their *vergiers* (the almost invariable appellation, which seems better translated as *garden* than the usual *orchard* or *grove*) nevertheless vary considerably even though most of their details have counterparts in the *Roman de la Rose*. Thus, in Machaut's *Behaingne*, the two mournful lovers appear in a *petit destour* beside a brook to which the poet has been led by a bird. In *Remede de Fortune* the vision of Esperence is experienced beside a spring in a walled garden; and the young knight and the narrator in the *Fonteinne amoreuse* see Venus and the knight's beloved beside the pool of Narcissus in another enclosed *parc*. In *Dit dou Lyon* the whole series of strange and miraculous events takes place in the *vergier* cut off from the mainland by an unfathomable river. The setting for *Navarre* is the woods where the narrator is hunting—not, exceptionally, a place apart, but nevertheless the realm of Flora and Zephirus.

There is no enumeration of plants and trees in the *Duchess* in the manner of Guillaume de Lorris, whose Amant in the Garden of Deduit finds and names vegetation from far and near (ll. 1323-74, 1399-1410). But Chaucer's failure to catalogue the flowers and trees was quite in line with the practice of Guillaume de Machaut and other poets of the genre (who nevertheless often enumerated species of birds as Chaucer does not in the *Duchess*). Froissart's *Paradys d'Amours* alone furnishes a notable list of flowers, in the *balade* to the daisy which later provided a source for the Prologue to the *Legend of Good Women*.[16] There are no significant lists of trees outside of the *Rose*. The properties of the unspecified trees of the *Duchess*, which are fifty fathoms high, only ten or twelve feet apart, with leaves not an inch asunder so

that no sunlight comes through, are taken directly from the *Rose*.
Chaucer does enumerate several animals in this poem. There
are notable lists also in the *Dit dou Lyon* and the *Panthère
d'Amours*,[17] but these consist more of jungle animals than of the
gentler game that Chaucer names. His list is analogous with the
briefer catalogue of Guillaume de Lorris:

> Ou vergier ot dains e chevriaus;
> S'i ot grant plenté d'escuriaus,
> Qui par ces arbres gravissoient;
> Conins i avoit, qui issoient
> Toute jor hors de lor tesnieres.   (*Rose*, ll. 1375-79)

> And many an hert and many an hynde
> Was both before me and behynde.
> Of founes, sowres, bukkes, does
> Was ful the woode, and many roes,
> And many sqwirelles, that sete
> Ful high upon the trees and ete,
> And in hir maner made festes.   (*Duchess*, ll. 427-433)

Magically these animals multiply in Chaucer's poem till Argus
could not number them on his counter; then they disperse "doun
the wood" as if frightened by the sudden appearance of the
narrator, who in turn now sees the Black Knight with his back to
an oak.

The narrator's tree in the *Duchess*, beside which he was
evidently stationed for the hunt,[18] is hardly one of the special
trees which is likely to play a part in the events of the *dits
amoreux*; but the "ook, an huge tree" (l. 447), against which the
Black Knight has his back when first seen, certainly qualifies.
The original of these is the pine of the *Roman de la Rose* which
towers above the pool of Narcissus, more beautiful than any seen
since the time of Charlemagne and Pepin (ll. 1427-29). Comparably, the dreamer of *Paradys d'Amours* finds himself in a fair
wood, in which he wanders up and down till he comes to a
particularly beautiful place beside a stream, where he makes his

23

complaint under a full-blown hawthorn. In Watriquet's *Dit de l'Arbre royal*, the magnificent tree provides the title subject for the poem, and the pear tree does the same thing for Thibaut's *Romanz de la Poire*. In Jean de Condé's *Messe des oisiaus* and Raimon Vidal's *Chasse aux médisants*[19] the narrators sit under single, leafy trees of unnamed species.

In the *Rose* the pool of Narcissus lies beneath the pine. While the oak in the *Duchess* parallels the pine of the *Rose*, there is no counterpart to the pool of Narcissus; in Machaut's *dits*, on the other hand, though a *fonteinne* or stream is generally found, particular trees are not singled out. The narrator of *Behaingne* sits under plural, unspecified trees; he stations himself within a hedge of eglantine in *Remede de Fortune*; a statue rises up beside the spring in *Fonteinne amoreuse*, taking the place of the pine; and it is the tent of the princess which is beside the pool in *Dit dou Lyon*.

Like the pool beneath the great tree in the *Rose*, the huge oak in the *Duchess* marks the end of a lengthy introduction. After the main stories begin there are only derivative and decorative congruencies between the two works. Before this the dream sequence, as has been shown, is very similar in the two poems. The considerable portion of the introduction of the *Duchess* which precedes the dream, however, is mostly indebted to Froissart and Machaut—to Froissart's *Paradys d'Amours* for the narrator's sleeplessness and the process of going to sleep, and to Machaut's *Fonteinne amoreuse* for the story of Seys and Alcyone.[20] But these poems with their short introductions clearly do not provide a precedent for the complication of the whole prologue—what Manly calls the "long and tortuous corridors" through which Chaucer leads his reader "before he arrives at the real subject."[21] The most relevant precedent for his technique of introduction is, again, the *Roman de la Rose*.

In both Guillaume's *Rose* and the *Duchess* approximately one-third of the work is occupied with material prefatory to the central narrative. Perhaps because Guillaume places most of his

24

introduction within the dream, the structure of his narrative has not puzzled critics as has the structure of the *Duchess*.[22] In both poems, however, the prefatory parts have an organic relationship to the narratives in that they serve to develop the subjects with which the narratives are to deal. The introductory sections of the *Roman de la Rose* consist mainly of a series of scenes—in which, for the most part, the narrator is a spectator—which help to define the subject matter of the story that follows. He sees a group of abstractions of things excluded from the garden, then a group of abstractions which inhabit the garden, and subsequently various activities and components of the garden, one of these elements being the pool of Narcissus which at length provides an appropriate focus for the commencement of the story. In the opening part of Chaucer's poem, likewise, the narrator witnesses a series of scenes. But while Guillaume introduces his narrative through visual definition of the subject, Chaucer develops his by analogy; the dreamer's plight, the Seys and Alcyone story, the unsuccessful hunt, even the references to the stories of Troy and the *Rose* itself, all foreshadow and provide parallels to the plight of the Black Knight.

The method of introduction in each poem is appropriate to the subject. Romantic love is a fascinating and protean phenomenon which is susceptible of minute exposition; thus, development by definition is quite suitable to the *Rose*. Death, on the other hand, the subject of the *Duchess*, is an overpowering phenomenon, whose oppressiveness one shuns. Chaucer's several parallels of loss and tragedy delicately prepare the reader—and the one to be consoled—for the ultimate statement of the fact. In the body of the poem Chaucer follows up the tactful introduction by not clearly revealing the death of Blanche till the end of the work.[23]

That Chaucer was conscious of his introductory section as a structural entity is attested to by his use of comparable indirect but functional introductions in the *House of Fame* and the *Parliament of Fowls*. It seems clear that Chaucer adapted the technique of the long, indirect introductions from Guillaume de

Lorris, despite some differences in approach. Even the treatment of the Seys and Alcyone exemplum seems to derive more from the story of Narcissus in the *Rose* than from Machaut, though the latter is the immediate source. Chaucer tells the story for the same overt reason as Machaut—to exemplify the power of Morpheus—but Chaucer pulls the story out front, where it also operates, and more importantly, in developing the main subject. The Ovidian story of Narcissus in the *Rose* likewise precedes the main narrative and serves a multiple function; the story suggests the nature of the love to be dealt with, and the rejection of Echo by Narcissus presents a parallel to the later repulses which Amant receives. Machaut by contrast tells the story of Seys and Alcyone in the midst of his poem, with the main events of the exemplum, the deaths of the protagonists, having no relevance to the main narrative of *Fonteinne*. Machaut, furthermore, retains the metamorphosis of Seys and Alcyone from the original, whereas both Chaucer and Guillaume de Lorris simplify their stories, substituting death for metamorphosis, thus eliminating material extrinsic to their main business. The terminology by which they end their stories is remarkably similar:

"Allas!" quod she [Alcyone] for sorwe,
And deyede within the thridde morwe.   (ll. 213-214)

Il [Narcissus] perdi d'ire tot le sen
Et fu morz en poi de termine."   (ll. 1503-04)

There are two other notable examples of lengthy indirect introductions among the poems dealt with in this study. The *Romanz de la Poire*, after twenty dedicatory lines in octosyllabic couplets, has a series of eleven twenty-line strophes in alexandrine couplets. These strophes consist chiefly of monologues by sundry figures: Amor vaunts his power; Fortune says that she passes out delight to loyal lovers and evil to the disloyal; Cligés addresses Fenice; Tristan tells how Mark found him asleep with Iseult in a cave with a sword between them; an allegorical love battle is

26

narrated; and the names of Paris and Helen are invoked as a testimony to the power of Amor. This series is related in subject to the subsequent conventional love story of the main narrative, but the connecting figure of the narrator-lover found in Chaucer and Guillaume de Lorris is lacking, and the essential cogency of the individual examples to the main story seems vague. An entirely different kind of beginning is found in Machaut's *Jugement dou Roy de Navarre*. In the first 460 lines of this poem the poet tells about his thoughts while he sits in his chamber during the disagreeable weather of November 1349. He considers the bad signs in the heavens which have caused calamitous earthquakes, and he thinks of other unfortunate events: the poisoning of drinking water by the Jews and their severe punishments, and the unnatural practices of flagellation which have become notorious. Such acts have caused Nature to send storms and the Plague, the Plague supplying the reason for the poet's staying locked in his room. The story that follows this introduction tells how, with the Plague scare ended, the poet rides out hunting and becomes involved in a love-debate with Bonneurté. Though a certain connection may be found between the report of the Plague and the debate, in the fact that they both are concerned with the deaths of loved ones,[24] the primary effect of the juxtaposition of these accounts is that of contrast of subject and scene. There is little similarity between this introductory section and that of the *Duchess*.

Thus the *Roman de la Rose* provides the most direct source for several matters of narrative, detail, and structure of the *Book of the Duchess*. The action involving Chaucer's narrator from his awakening in a dream to his encountering the Black Knight by a great oak, and the description of the birds and the garden are based on Guillaume's work. So, likewise, is the technique of the long introduction, in which are combined scenes and minor narratives that serve to develop the main subject of the poem and are tied together as experiences of the narrator, who is a chief character in the whole poem. In the main, however, the *Roman*

27

de la Rose is a more distant ancestor of Chaucer's poem. It will be well to summarize some of the differences between the two works in order to bring out some broader considerations with which this study concerns itself.

One essential and striking difference between the two is the nature of the participants. Guillaume de Lorris' poem is inhabited by personifications of qualities and forces such as Deduit, Oiseuse, Dangier, and Amor, and by persons with abstract names who operate in a one-sided fashion, such as Ami, Malebouche, and the narrator (as Amant). But no main characters in the *Duchess* are personifications, and the active people are reasonably well-rounded figures: the narrator is a lover, a reader, a huntsman, and an adviser, with a rather humorous personality; the Black Knight is a hunter, a king with a castle, and a lover; the lady is a paragon not only of amorous virtue, but also of virtue in general. The only personifications in Chaucer's work are those found in the speeches of the Black Knight: Love, Yowthe, Fortune, and Nature. Of these only Fortune has any prominence.

In the nature of the actions is found a further essential difference. The actions of the two poems are similar at the beginning, to be sure, with each narrator making a series of observations, though the observations of the narrator in the *Rose* effect an allegorical process of education and conditioning which does not take place in the *Duchess*. The modes of the central narrative sharply differ. In the *Rose* psychological allegory is used to represent the process of falling in love and the lover's successive advances and repulses. The Knight of the *Duchess*, on the other hand, merely states that he was a servant of Love and was governed in idleness by Yowthe, these statements involving short metaphors rather than the continued metaphors which constitute allegory. Only one passage of Chaucer's poem is allegorical in the way that Guillaume de Lorris' poem is allegorical, that in which the Knight describes how Fortune played chess with him and won his queen (ll. 652-684). Otherwise, the actions, like the characters, may be seen as realistic.

28

Another significant—if not quite so basic—difference lies in the fact that the narrator is the central figure throughout the *Roman de la Rose*, while in the elegy of the *Duchess* the role of the narrator recedes to a secondary importance. The type of love which is involved in the two poems is quite different too. The lover of Guillaume's poem clearly longs for, and is intent on, physical conquest of the lady. At the same time the love of the Black Knight for his idealized lady seems to be of a transcendent kind—physical contact is not in question. And of course the love affairs are at contrasting stages: one lady has repulsed her lover, the other lady has died. This means that the business of the two poems must be different: in the one case the lover claims to write his poem as an appeal to the lady; in the other case the narrator wishes to comfort the Knight, the poet to comfort John of Gaunt.

How Chaucer's characters came to be people rather than abstractions, and how his action came to be a realistic one rather than an allegory of the mind, are important questions for this study, which historical developments help to explain. Precedents for most of the other significant differences between the *Roman de la Rose* and the *Book of the Duchess* are also found in the development of the *dit amoreux*. The next two chapters will deal with works written between the time of Guillaume de Lorris and Guillaume de Machaut. While these have only a minor direct relationship to the *Book of the Duchess*, their relevance to the development which produced Chaucer's first long original poem is crucial.

CHAPTER II

THE CENTRALIZED ALLEGORIES

In the preceding chapter I postulated a division of Guillaume's *Roman de la Rose* into three parts. First there is the Maytime walk to and through the Garden of Deduit, during which the narrator makes some detailed observations of scenes of nature and of two allegorical tableaux. In this section the narrator is primarily a spectator. In the second part the narrator has a series of love experiences, which are expressed in three allegorical cadres: the pool, the rose-garden, and the God of Love's assault and capture of him (which entails a lengthy lecture). Here the allegorical framework is manipulated freely, and that which may properly be called psychological allegory is only rudimentarily present, notably in the arrows of Amour. The third part is devoted to a full-blown psychological allegory, involving a fragmentation of the psyches of both lover and beloved and an analysis of the forces at work on them. The cadre of this allegory is stabilized with its locale being centralized.

The French love narratives which followed the *Rose* tend to be modelled on one of the three parts of their progenitor. Some of these consist simply of a sequence of observations by the narrator, including allegorical scenes, often under the conduct of a guide (found in the *Rose* in the person of Oiseuse). Others tell a love story in which the main character passes through a series of conventional experiences, often expressed in convenient and shifting allegorical frames. Narratives of the third sort are well-developed psychological allegories which personifications dominate, centered around a single aspect of courtly activity. Guillaume de Lorris constructs his narrative around the rose garden and castle enclosure, while his successors make use of the prison, the law process, and particularly the hunt. This chapter deals with centralized stories which resemble in form Guillaume's third section. The French narratives comparable to the first two parts of the *Rose* will be taken up in the next chapter.

Four *dits amoreux* written between the time of Guillaume de Lorris and Guillaume de Machaut have psychological allegories which are developed around a central framework: Baudouin de Condé's *Prisons d'Amours*, whose title suggests its setting; Philippe de Remi's *Salu d'Amours*, which takes place in a law court; and two love hunts, the *Dis dou cerf amoreus*, and Jehan Acart's *Prise amoreuse*. Raimon Vidal's *Chasse aux médisants*, though barely allegorical, is a centralized love hunt and will be treated in this chapter. All five of these poems tend to fulfill, better than the other poems in the tradition, the modern critical requirement of organic unity, since their narrative frameworks are stable and the stories are developed within these frameworks. At the same time, however, two factors tend to detract from their literary value. In the first place the very tendency which leads the poet to adopt a single allegorical scheme sometimes leads him to adhere too rigidly to this scheme. Guillaume de Lorris expands his rose garden into a whole castle ground without radically changing the cadre and without interfering with the progression of his psychological narrative. He is thus able to introduce new and interesting features into his allegorical landscape. But Guillaume's imitators generally lack his ability to freely improvise while adhering to the adopted scheme. Secondly, none of the poets except perhaps Jehan Acart is able to match Guillaume's facility in simulating the interplay between lover and beloved and their separate reactions through two sets of personifications and abstractions. With the other poets the lover's psyche is the main concern of the allegory, while the lady gets only perfunctory attention.

31

Another defect exhibited by some of these works results from the poet's glossing of his own allegory. Guillaume de Lorris never stops to explain the meaning of his allegory. The world in which his personifications live whirls on its own axis without the impediment of glosses. Some later writers, on the other hand, feel constrained to halt their narratives periodically to explain what they mean, a step which inevitably impairs the poetic effect of their imaginative worlds. In *Prisons d'Amours*, written between 1240 and 1280, Baudouin de Condé explicitly applies every stage in the description of the fictional lover's progress through Love's prison to his own ostensibly non-fictional affair.[1] This necessitates frequent shifting from the story to the gloss, a factor which led William Neilson to characterize the poem as "a long and tedious allegorical poem," interrupted by "frequent digressions."[2] Neilson's evaluation is perhaps justified on the several counts already named, but nevertheless Baudoin's creation and insistent carrying through of his original allegorical scheme imparts a sense of organization to his narrative which increases as the poem progresses, and his treatise on the five ways to escape from love's prison is genuinely entertaining.

At the beginning of this 3131-line work, Baudouin says that he will describe the Prison of Love whose tortures no dungeon of king, duke, or count can match. He entreats Amour to help him write a poem which will please his lady; and he tells the *mesdisans* not to gape because he calls a married lady *ma dame*, for he is not writing for him. The poet goes on to explain that Amour, like any other lord, has a prison. This prison is built on a foundation of beauty, goodness, and the other qualities which a mistress should possess. It has two floors; the lower floor is filled with great tribulation, the upper with joy. The eyes and ears provide the road to the doorway, which is constructed of Sweet Hope. Fortune with her wheel is stationed inside the tower where she oftentimes carries the ugly, the *nice*, and the good-for-nothings up high, while casting down the goodlooking, the wealthy, and the *vaillans*. "Hé las!" cries the poet: while he thought by merit to

32

ascend, he was cast down where unfortunate lovers are bitten by the little serpents of Sweet Memory, and by various other reptiles named Desire, Despair, and Fear of Failing.

Having reached the point in the allegory to which his own love has progressed, the poet intends to stop, but his lady commands him to continue. Thus, though he feels like a blind man without a guide, he goes on to describe (ll. 1736-2449) the possible ways of escape from the prison.

Not all who escape Love's prison, says the poet, leave it the same way: some tunnel out, some climb out the top, some are helped to get out by friends, and the relatives of others help them escape. Those of a fifth kind petition their lords until their releases are ordered. The first sort, those who tunnel out, are the ones who have such good control of themselves that they manage to forget their ladies. He who wishes thus to draw away from the lady ought to divert himself with a selling trip to England or Frisia, or—if he is wealthy—with hounds, falcons, chess, and tables; or he can play *marelle* at the tavern. As for himself, brags the poet, he cannot choose this way, for the foundation of his castle is too strong in beauty, goodness, and nobility. Escapees of the second type, who climb out the top, are those who cultivate an acquaintanceship with other ladies. The third sort allow their friends to convince them that it is foolish to spend time on ill-disposed women. The families of the fourth kind arrange marriages for them, and of necessity they forget their beloveds for their wives, since their former mistresses will not esteem them when they find out about their marriage. The poet is quick to add here that marriage is no excuse for a woman, for she would be wrong to desert her lover on account of her husband:

Mal ait qui pour mari
Laist son loial ami! (ll. 2309-10)

The fifth means, says the narrator, is the only way he will ever choose to escape: he will depend on the eventual efficacy of his prayers to bring him up on the Wheel of Fortune.

33

The remainder of the poem (ll. 2450-3131) tells how, when Amour eventually pricks the beloved with a golden dart, the lover is moved to the upper floor in four carefully-defined stages, the third stage being marked by Amoreuse Souffrance, which may lead the lady to grant the lover a token, such as a ring, a glove, or a belt. The final stage is reached when the lady deigns at length to grant him "un seul baisier"; then the lover will have been brought through the entrance of the "haut estage." After the lover has tested the lady's kisses, the poet advises him to work so that he may experience the other delights of *violetes* and *lis*, the violets standing for "le deduit de la pucelette," and the lilies for the pleasure of chambers and beds. As for the narrator, he claims to hope only for a kiss.

Having brought the allegory to an end, the poet extols the value of this poem as a gift, for other gifts are mute—a knight's prowess really adds nothing to the lady's glory, though he should win the prizes of thirty tournaments and fifteen Round Tables. But her praises will live in this *lai* always. Finally, the poet asserts that the lady's name is revealed anagrammatically in one of the final lines (it is yet undeciphered), and he asks Amour to tell the lady the truth of his love. Though the manuscript breaks off before the end of the work, there is evidently very little missing.

Baudouin's poem, written within fifty years of Guillaume de Lorris' work and probably before Jean de Meun's continuation, undoubtedly found its inspiration in the *Roman de la Rose*, though the details are not as thoroughly derivative from that poem as are those of many subsequent *dits amoreux*. The central metaphor of the prison of love, though a natural love metaphor which is not limited to the thirteenth- and fourteenth-century poems studied here, probably grew out of the God of Love's imprisonment of the lover's heart in Guillaume de Lorris' story. In the *Rose*, when the God of Love has wounded Amant with his arrow, Amant willingly becomes Love's prisoner:

34

E se de moi vostre prison
Volez faire ne ne deigniez,
Ne m'en tieng pas a engigniez.   (ll. 1914-16)

To enforce the captivity of Amant the God of Love literally imprisons his heart with a key (ll. 2008-10). Later Bel Acueil is also put in "prison" (ll. 4104, 4123), in this case the prison of Jalosie. The simile which Amour uses in his instructions to the lover, when he compares the plight of the civil prisoner to that of Love's prisoner, also is related to the *Prisons d'Amours*:

Cil que l'en met en chartre oscure,
En verminier e en ordure,
Qui n'a que pain d'orge ou d'avoine,
Ne se muert mie por la poine:
Esperance confort li livre,
E se cuide veoir delivre
Encor par aucune cheance;
Trestoute autretele beance
A cil qu'Amors tient en prison:
Il espoire sa guerison.   (ll. 2611-20)

The imprisonment of Bel Acueil, and of Guillaume's and Baudouin's lovers, is an integral part of the narratives. In later works, however, the prison is used only as an image. A particularly likely place for such a metaphor is in the lover's complaint, as when in Machaut's *Fonteinne amoreuse* the lover moans that the lady holds his heart in prison (ll. 779-794). In the *Remede de Fortune* of the same poet Amant complains that Amour scourges him in his prison; one ought not to beat the one he has conquered, he says, but rather ought to heal him (ll. 1225-40). Chaucer also found occasion to use the image; the third roundel of his *Merciles Beaute*, for example, centers on this metaphor, which is thrice repeated:

Sin I fro Love escaped am so fat,
I never thenk to ben in his prison lene;
Sin I am free, I counte him not a bene.   (ll. 27-29)

The process by which the Lover's imprisonment progresses from a literal status in the *Rose* to conventional metaphor in fourteenth-century narratives is perhaps indicated by Baudouin's dilution of his allegory with glosses. When the poets began to leaven their allegories with references to the real-life stories which the allegories referred to, the tendency for "real life" to assume precedence, and for the allegory to be reduced to the level of diction, seems to have become very strong. With Guillaume de Lorris the allegorical representation occupies the whole stage; with Baudouin de Condé the allegorical prison and the real lover's problem with the lady share the stage; and with Machaut and Chaucer the image is merely a conventional part of the dialogue, the realistic narrative having taken over completely.

Baudouin's allegory, like the other love narratives considered here, was based on a familiar aspect of medieval life. Prisons were commonly located in the lower levels of the castles, in which the unfortunate inmates would rot in the company of vermin, while one or two levels above a luxurious court life might be carried on in feasting, dancing, and pleasant rest between soft sheets. Another familiar feature of life which was used in love allegories was the court process, presided over by a king or nobleman.[3] Most of the numerous love narratives and allegories involving the courts depict simple decrees and decisions made by the judge, sometimes with the aid of advisers. In Machaut's *Behaingne* and *Navarre*, the king holds court *ad hoc* to decide *demandes d'amours*, and in Chaucer's Prologue to the *Legend of Good Women* the God of Love comes right into the garden to judge and pronounce sentence on the poet. Sometimes the proceeding is more formal. The most elaborate representation of a legal process among the *dits amoreux* is found, as seems natural, in a work of Philippe de Remi, Sire de Beaumanoir (c. 1250-96), whose very important legal writings have far overshadowed his work as a poet.[4]

As also might be expected of the product of a legal mind, in Philippe's *Salu d'Amours* the allegory is worked out with considerable order, logic, and consistency. He does not interrupt his allegorical presentation with digressions or explanations, and at the same time he avoids the dryness which is often another product of the lawyer's discipline. The 1048-line *Salu d'Amours* was probably composed before 1280, perhaps very near the time of *Prisons d'Amours.*

In the dedication the poet says he sends these verses to his lady by the instruction of Amours in the hope that she will help him out of his troubles. At a *carole* one day, the poet goes on to relate (ll. 121 ff.), Amours (a female in this poem) strikes him with her arrow through the eye into the heart. Subsequently, Orguel and Cointise seize him and Traison requires him to surrender, for he had taken a lady by the finger without having first entered into the goddess' service. Amours orders him to the prison of Pensée, and calls for an immediate trial. Unfortunately for the lover all the bad counsellors of Amours are in court— Orguel, Fole Cointise, Envie, Felonie, and Mesdis—but Loiauté, Pitié, Franchise, Deboinnairté, and Esperance are unable to come at the moment. Amours wants to wait for the testimony of Loiauté, but Traison, glozing and flattering, convinces the lover that he should put all his trust in him. Since it is acceptable to the accused, Amours lets Traison pronounce judgment.

Philippe, it may be observed, works out the allegory thoughtfully throughout the poem. The lover's reliance on Traison in the trial, for example, represents allegorically the resort by the lover to tactics contrary to the accepted rules of the game of love. For this he pays dearly, for Traison, having consulted his fellow-ruffians, prescribes ten penalties (ll. 461-674). The lover is to remain in the prison of Pensée for the rest of his life, sigh without ceasing, fear failure seven days a week, lie awake, toss and turn, always long for his lady's company, have her face in his thought constantly, be always jealous, tremble continually, and always despair of obtaining mercy. Traison and his cohorts are very well satisfied with this verdict, but when they see Loiauté and her group enter, without taking leave they skulk away to the court

37

of France where they are well-loved (The poet adds that if he did not fear the king he would speak more of this matter).

Now (l. 675) the lover kneels weeping and tells the good counsellors of Amour how Traison has betrayed him; they in turn kneel before Amours and ask some relief for him. Amours agrees that the punishment is harsh, but notes that the lover has been rash in putting his trust in Traison. She accedes to Loiauté's suggestion that while the ten penalties sould be inflicted as prescribed, they should be terminated at the pleasure of the lady, and that Pitié and Franchise should remind the lady of his sufferings, and Esperance should comfort him. Loiauté further bids the lover not to be morose if his relief does not come quickly; in the meanwhile he should write amorous *dits* and *chansons* to his mistress describing his love. It is in accordance with this last instruction, the poet concludes, that he has undertaken to put this *salu* in rhyme, and he prays that his lady will remit his pains by granting her love:

> Vous requier je d'amors le don
> Et pri cent mile fois merci. (ll. 1004-05)

The connection of Philippe's narrative with that of the *Roman de la Rose* shows up in the sequence at the beginning of *Salu* when Amours shoots the lover and demands his surrender. Several of the personifications, furthermore, have counterparts in Guillaume de Lorris' work: Envie, Mesdis, Loiauté, Pitié, Franchise, and Esperance. But the prominence of a new figure, Traison, is interesting. In Guillaume de Lorris' poem the lover is told to honor and treat ladies well, not for reasons of morality, but so that they will speak and think well of him. Guillaume might say that improper tactics involve bad judgment, but he would not classify them as criminal. Although he probably would not have gone so far as to introduce into his story a successful hypocrite such as Jean de Meun's Faus Semblant, nevertheless success in love rather than honorable action is his preoccupation. In Philippe's poem the tendency can be seen, which became stronger in the *dits amoreux*, for questions of the morality of Amour to figure prominently and for the nature of the *merci* and *pitié* which the lover seeks to be hidden under an idealized rhetoric. In the later poems the lover would not presume to dream that he had his lady naked in bed, as the God of Love depicts him dreaming in the *Rose*, nor can he openly aspire to the pleasures of the lily, as is suggested in the *Prisons d'Amours*. Proper behavior in love replaces proper strategy as the dominant concern of the narratives, one rule of proper behavior demanding that the lover be modest in his expectations and not desire anything which would impair the lady's honor. A result is that all kinds of love between the sexes become appropriate subjects for the *dits amoreux* — innocent premarital love, illicit extramarital love, and the married love which lies behind Machaut's *Fonteinne amoreuse* and Chaucer's *Duchess*.

Courts were a common feature in love poetry through the fifteenth century, as Professor Neilson's study has shown, but there is no law process depicted which is as elaborate as that in Philippe's *Salu d'Amours*, and none of the other poems relevant to this study uses the court as the central feature of its narrative. Another aspect of medieval activity, the hunt, provided the cadre for several love allegories. The other three poems to be taken up in this chapter are all organized around love hunts, the anonymous *Dis dou cerf amoreus*, Jehan Acart de Hesdin's *Prise amoreuse*, and Raimon Vidal's *Chasse aux médisants*.

These three works have a marked resemblance to each other in the prominence given to allegorized hunting dogs. This fact also marks the poems as being related to some Middle High German allegories of the chase, in which, as Neilson describes them, "the woman is represented by the prey, and the dogs and other accompaniments of the hunt are the qualities and devices used to win her."[5] The whole group no doubt received important inspiration from the hunt in the *Roman de la Rose* in which the God of Love himself is the huntsman and the dreamer is his prey.

The first extant French poem to develop the love-hunt, and

perhaps a progenitor of the German works as well as of its French successors, is the short (326-line) *Cerf amoreus*, written between 1250 and 1300.[6] This poem is only secondarily an allegory, since the personified love chase is presented simply as an elaborate comparison suggested to the narrator by his witnessing an actual hunt of a deer followed by the slaughtering of it.[7] The narrator muses that one has to pursue a lady with as much assiduity as he does a deer; Amours is like the teacher and leader of the dogs who pursue the *cerf amoreus*, the lady. From this point the narrator develops the simile in his mind into a complete narrative. When the lady is attracted by a man, she takes refuge in the bushes of her pride, and it is then that Amours must bring up his dogs. First, the hound Pensée, baying *trebles*, *motets*, and *chansons*, flushes the deer into the open field, for when the lady thinks of the long time her lover has honored her, she is bitten and torn by such thoughts and leaves her place of pride. But in order to keep the deer out in the open other dogs are necessary, and Souvenirs, who has been coupled with Pensée, comes up. Then Desirriers and Voluntés, also coupled together, are released. But the *cerf*, fearful of *mesdisants*, runs off to find some water, and it finally takes another pair of hounds, Humilités and Pitiés, to bring the deer to its knees. The dogs joyfully feed and bathe themselves in the blood of the deer. Likewise the *amant* has great joy when the lady grants her love.

In the *Cerf amoreus* the explanations are so elaborate that the allegory of the chase is reduced to a series of similes. Such is not the case with Jehan Acart de Hesdin's *Prise amoreuse*,[8] written about a half-century later (1332), where the allegory is mostly left to speak for itself. In this poem the cleric's scholastic education perhaps manifests itself in the extent to which Jehan carries out the allegory, though this does not inhibit him from making his allegorical scheme somewhat inconsistent when it suits him.[9] The 1951 lines which at latest count make up the work[10] include nine *balades* and nine *rondeaux* interspersed throughout, with one of the *balades* at the beginning of the poem and one at the end.

These lyrics are not part of the narrative, but rather fortify the sentiments expressed in the story. The lover rather than the beloved is the prey in the *Prise amoreuse*, in accordance with the scheme of the hunt in the *Roman de la Rose*, and reversing that of the *Cerf amoreus*. The allegorical details are nevertheless worked out in a manner similar to *Cerf amoreus*, though more elaborately.

Jean proclaims at the beginning that he writes the poem in honor of his lady. He relates that in April, 1332, Nature so operates in him that she lifts the shadows of his youthful ignorance (though he was not so mature that he "looked for Reason" in his actions, ll. 116-117) and places him in the *bois de jonece*. In this wood, which is always covered with dewy green grass and filled with beautiful trees, are four roads called Leece, Compaignie, Cointise, and Fol Cuidier. One stays on these roads till old age robs him of leaf and fruit; then all roads fail. Thus by right of age the poet enters the Wood of Jonece (ll. 281 ff.) and delights in the pleasant road of Leece; his senses are still under his control. But Amours, his people, and their dogs are out hunting. Amours has with him Renon and Los, Maniere and Courtoisie, Voloir and Plaisance; in the road of Fol Cuidier he has Samblant and Espoir, and all about this way stretches the net of Desir. Amours uncouples Biauté and the first of the poet's senses, Regars, is caught like the tiger which in looking at himself in a mirror forgets to protect himself and is taken by the hunters. Avis warns Regars against being caught by Amours, and Regars reluctantly flees till he enters the road of Compaignie.

The allegorical scheme is now quite complicated, but Jehan handles it rather neatly. It involves three major groups of abstractions: qualities attached to the lady, represented by personified hunting dogs; the senses of the lover, who is the main object of the hunt; and the various roads of the Wood of Youth, which represent the stages of courtship. As the story proceeds (l. 689) Regars is joined by the poet's hearing, Oir, who is blandished with the praises of the lady by the hounds Renon and Los. The melody of David and Orpheus, thinks Oir, is discordant in comparison with the baying of these dogs. Ignorance now causes Regars and Oïr to flee back to the Bush of Enfance in which the poet is hidden, where they tell the heart what they have seen and found. Amours sends Penser and Souvenir who carefully detail to the heart the lady's physical attractions (ll. 906-1010). Gouster and Toucher are excited by the description, and each desires to perform his function. To make things worse Penser jumps on the incipient lover and bites him *griefment*, upon which he leaps out of the bush, and then is very frightened, for he has left his safe retreat.

After praising the lady and pleading for her pity it occurs to the lover that Amours has betrayed him by making him aim too high, for he is to his mistress as tin to gold. He flees to the road named Cointise, where he disports till attacked by Pleasance, Voloir, Souvenir, Penser, and Renons. His senses refuse to flee and all the dogs of Amours run upon him and seize the senses. Espoirs tells the lover that if he does his duty he will obtain grace, which heartens him to exclaim rapturously that he surrenders to the beautiful one, the fountain of all joys. But Doutance comes up and warns him that, "If the appearance is lovely and demure, the heart is proud and unyielding" (ll. 1520-21). When the lover now hesitates for fear of failing, all the dogs of Amours attack and bite him. *Par force* he is driven into the road of Cuidier, where he runs into the net of Desir in which the more he struggles the more he is caught. Amours, disposing of the prey as is proper, divides him in three parts: he reserves the body for himself, gives the dogs the entrails to eat and the blood to drink, while the lady gets the heart. The poet concludes by begging his lady's pardon for having fled from her at first, and he expresses hope for her *merci*.

The careful and elaborate development of the psychological allegory in the *Prise amoreuse* relates it more directly to the *dits* of Guillaume de Lorris, Philippe de Remi, and Baudouin de Condé, written in the previous century, than to its contemporaries. More characteristic in mode of the love poems of the 1330's is Raimon Vidal's *Chasse aux médisants*.[11] In this poem the hunters

42

are historical personages and there is no allegorical narrative for the personifications to operate in.

The beginning of the *Chasse aux médisants* is reminiscent of the *Cerf amoreus*. The poet is sitting under a large, leafy tree, thinking of his lady, when his reverie is interrupted by a crowd of men approaching with spears, darts, and lances. Many men are leading dogs and many women are mounted and have horns about their necks. Gaston de Lille, leading the group, greets the poet by name and introduces him to the Count of Foix and his brother, Bertrand. Gaston explains that the hunting party—which includes such noblewomen as the Countess of Erminac, Gaston's wife Marguerite, and the Viscountess of Biaumont—set out the day before on a hunt for *mesdisans*. He then (l. 113) tells the story of the *sangler* which they are presently intent on killing. This *porc* used to be a great and powerful man who slandered everyone, including a handsome young man and worthy lady who had to separate as a result of his calumny. The young man in consequence of the enforced separation took to his bed, where he prayed the *Diex d'Amours* to let his power and vengeance fall on the slanderer. Answering the prayer, the god turned the envious lord into a wild boar right in the middle of his castle, so that he had to flee from his servants into the woods. He has been in these woods a hundred years now, Gaston concludes, which is the term fixed by the god, so now he must be hunted down and killed.

Each of the seventeen ladies gives instructions and encouragement to her brace of dogs; e.g., Blanche de Foys instructs Biaumaintien and Douregart, and Sevilla de Chastiauneuf addresses her *levriers*, Bonté and Grace. One dog, called Bonnefoy, who is white as snow, hunts singly and unattended. Now the dogs are released (l. 509) and the ladies urge them on. Each of the four noblest women guards a quarter of the wood outside with her dogs. As the boar is flushed from the wood Bertrand strikes him. The dogs chase him and the Count de Foix deals him another blow with the spear. At this point, "par trop grant merveille," the boar makes an oration, confessing that he was a *mesdisans* all his life and so entertains no hope for mercy. Each of the thirteen gentlemen, now named, strikes the *sangler*, who at length expires. Gaston divides the four quarters of the boar among the ladies who guarded outside, gives the tongue to Bertrand, and reserves the heart of gall for himself to dispose of.

The scheme of the *Chasse aux médisants* is original in its making the quarry the slanderer rather than either of the lovers. The modern reader may find Raimon's version more suitable than a representation in which one of the lovers is torn by hounds, but the latter was standard. In the *Roman de la Rose* and the *Prise amoreuse* the man is the hunted, while in the *Cerf amoreus* and the several German *Jagdallegorien*[12] the lady is the game. The lady is also the hunted in Froissart's *Paradys d'Amours* where the hunt of love enters briefly into the story (ll. 903-953) as a kind of narrative decoration. As Amant is being guided through the countryside by Plaisance and Esperance they encounter a young man named Beaus Samblant, who is holding three hunting dogs; Douls Regards at the same time is blowing his horn. Plaisance explains that "In this season [May, of course] the God of Love pursues the chase. I don't know what game they are seeking at the moment; but there is no hour of the day that they take repose." She points out Franc Voloir, who likewise has three *levriers*. "Are all the hunters here in the service of Amour?" asks Amant. "And thirty times more," she answers; "counts, dukes, and kings, who enjoy the amorous chase, and each hunts where he thinks there is game."

How a full-scale allegory might be worked out from the details provided in this brief section of Froissart's poem is problematical. But the provenience of this sequence from the hunt of love tradition is manifest, and it is interesting in its providing the nearest analogue among the immediate sources of the *Book of the Duchess* for the hunting scene of that poem. The hunt in the *Duchess*, which takes place shortly after the dream begins (ll. 344-386), is easily the longest description of the chase in Chaucer's writings.[13] Ignorance evidently had nothing to do with

44

Chaucer's usual taciturnity on the subject, however, for, as Oliver F. Emerson has shown,[14] Chaucer speaks like an initiate in this passage, which involves realistic description rather than personifications or explicit allegory.

The dreamer, having heard a hunting horn and mounted men talking about their plans for killing the hart, jumps on his horse and rides out of his chamber. He overtakes a "gret route" of hunters and foresters, and finds that this is the party of Emperor Octavian, who is himself close at hand. When they come to the edge of the forest every man goes about his assigned part in the hunt, and the master of the hunt blows "thre mot" as the hounds are uncoupled. The halloos of the hunters shortly signal that the hart has been located, and it is pursued for a long time. Finally, however, the hart is lost:

> This hert rused, and staal away
> Fro alle the houndes a privy way.
> The houndes had overshote hym alle,
> And were on a defaute yfalle.
> Therwyth the hunte wonder faste
> Blew a forloyn at the laste. (ll. 381-386)

A little inexperienced puppy (he "koude no good"), who had tagged along to the hunt, now leads the narrator down the garden path away from the hunting grounds. The subject of the hunt is reintroduced passingly when the dreamer is trying to find a subject which will lead the knight to talk:

> "Sir," quod I, "This game is doon.
> I holde that this hert be goon;
> These huntes konne hym no wher see."
> "Y do no fors thereof," quod he;
> "My thought is theron never a del." (ll.539-543)

The knight then tells all about his troubles, and the hunt is only spoken of again at the conclusion of the poem. When the knight makes the final revelation of the lady's death, the dreamer responds,

45

> "Be God, hyt ys routhe!"
> And with that word ryght anoon
> They gan to strake forth; al was doon,
> For that tyme, the hert-huntyng.
> With that me thoghte that this kyng
> Gan homwardes for to ryde...[15]

There are no immediate sources for this hunting sequence in the *Duchess*. But though the poems of the tradition supply no verbal parallels, they do provide an insight into the function of the chase in Chaucer's poem, which is hardly that of a digressive interlude. Even without taking previous poems of the hunt into account, it is obvious that loss of the deer provides some kind of parallel to the knight's loss of his duchess.[16] And consideration of the tradition serves to make the parallel less tenuous.

The fact that the land in which Chaucer's dreamer goes hunting is the land of the *Roman de la Rose*—Love's bailiwick—along with the fact that there was a contemporary tradition of Hunt of Love poems (among them *Paradys d'Amours*, an important source of the *Duchess*), implies that Octavian's hunting party is in some sense engaged in a Hunt of Love. Chaucer's failure to allegorize the hunt explicitly enhances the potential significance of his short passage by allowing it to exist as effective natural description, and also to carry at least two allegorical implications. The first of these would figure the Black Knight as the Amant at the head of the hunt in pursuit of his beloved; the hart's disappearance by a "privy way," then, signifies her death. In the second place the Black Knight may be seen as the bereft Amant, sitting apart from the chase of Amour, no longer interested in what was once an all-absorbing sport to him: "My thought ys thereon never a del." The effect obtained by such implications is analogous with that achieved in *Sir Gawain and the Green Knight* by the pairing of the three chases with the three attempts at seduction. While in that poem an allegorization of the hunts identifies the knight with the prey rather than with the hunter as in the *Duchess*, a real similarity with the *Duchess* is

46

nevertheless found in the Gawain poet's insertion of realistic description of the chase into a story of Amour. In both poems the juxtaposition of these narrative elements makes it difficult to deny significance to the parallels of the events of the hunt with the events of the love story, especially in the light of the Hunt of Love tradition.

That tradition, of course, goes in both directions quite beyond the limits of this study. The mere fact that bow and arrow were standard equipment of the classical god of love indicates the venerableness of the hunt-of-love metaphor. Ovid uses the figure in several places, as Marcelle Thiébaux points out, and Wolfram von Eschenbach and Gottfried von Strassburg, among others, employ it in their early thirteenth-century works.[17] In later centuries, stimulated by the elaborate love allegories which have been considered in this chapter, the use of the hunting metaphor became even more common. In *Troilus and Criseyde*, for instance, Troilus taunts his love-struck comrades who have such great woe "when [their] prey is lost" (1. 201); later, he moans to himself, "O fool, now artow in the snare" (1. 507); Pandarus shortly thereafter tells Troilus how Love had caught even Phebus "in a snare" (1. 663); a few lines farther on Troilus considers that it is sometimes "craft to seme fle/Fro thyng whych in effect men hunte faste" (1. 747-748); and in the next book Pandarus promises Troilus that he "Shal wel the deer unto thi bowe dryve" (ll. 1535). Examples from *Troilus*, the remainder of Chaucer's work, and love poetry of all succeeding centuries accumulate indefinitely, including such delicate uses of it as Sir Thomas Wyatt's lament for his lost charm:

> They flee from me that sometime did me seek,
> With naked foot, stalking within my chamber.
> I have seen them gentle, tame, and meek,
> That now are wild, and do not once remember
> That sometime they put themselves in danger
> To take bread at my hand.

Other aspects of medieval court life, metaphorically applied to love, are also adaptable to full-scale allegories: the chess game, the castle, falconry, dicing, the highway, and the religious service. All of these were employed for allegory to some extent by the poets of the *dits amoreux*. Machaut built a long and unified, if dull, allegory around the falconry metaphor, in the *Dit de l'Alerion*, which will be discussed in Chapter IV. In general, though, the poets of the fourteenth century seem not to have had the interest, or the patience, necessary for carrying through elaborate allegories such as those built by Guillaume de Lorris around the rose garden, Baudouin de Condé around the prison, Philippe de Remi around the law court, and the poet of the *Cerf amoreus* and Jehan Acart around the hunt. Such allegorical frameworks came to be used for short episodes or bare skeletons of the more diffuse narratives which will be taken up in the next chapter.

CHAPTER III

THE EPISODIC NARRATIVES

As the last part of Guillaume de Lorris' story is constructed around an expanding rose garden, so the centralized allegories dealt with in the previous chapter are built around a framework of materials borrowed from a single phenomenon or phase of medieval life. Other *dits amoreux* in the tradition of the *Roman de la Rose* are more difficult to classify, but in general those which precede Machaut's work may be associated with either the first or middle section of Guillaume's poem. Both of these sections of the *Rose* are episodic, but the narrator in the first part is a spectator who witnesses a series of scenes and events which have only a loose connection, while in the second part the narrator is the central participant in a love narrative which is developed by a series of separate episodes.

In the beginning of the *Rose* the observations of the dreamer link together a series of scenes: a lovely river, a group of figures depicted on the wall of a garden, a lady attended by song-birds, a carole in the garden, and a grove of wonderful trees. Only a thin narrative connection binds these scenes together; what coherence they have is provided by the narrator's presence. Very much like this part in structure are three fourteenth-century *dits*: Watriquet de Couvin's *Fontaine d'Amours* and *Tournois des dames*, and Jean de Condé's *Messe des oisiaus*. As in the beginning of the *Rose*, the various scenes which comprise these poems are connected chiefly by the narrator's presence rather than by narrative development.

The episodic *dits* written in the thirteenth century, on the other hand, are basically of the type in which a series of separate incidents, mostly allegorigal or semi-allegorical in nature, join to make a love story. In these the narrator is usually the central participant. The middle section of Guillaume's poem provides the model for this sort of narrative. When the dreamer in the *Rose* arrives at the pool of Narcissus, he becomes involved in a shifting allegory in which the first stages of a love affair are represented by means of the crystals in the pool, then a bed of rose bushes, and finally the arrows of the God of Love. *Dits* which resemble in structure this section of the *Rose* include Thibaut's *Romanz de la Poire*; two closely related anonymous poems, the *Fablel dou Dieu d'Amours*, and *De Venus la Deese d'Amor*; and Nicole de Margival's *Dit de la Panthère d'Amours*.

Since the division of the two kinds of episodic *dits* follows chronology, it will be convenient to deal with them in the order of their composition. Stories of the first sort, those in which there is a narrative development, will be considered first, and those which rely for their coherence on the narrator will then be taken up.

The *Romanz de la Poire*[1] is perhaps the earliest of the episodic poems, being written between 1230 and 1272, that is, after Guillaume de Lorris finished his section of the *Roman de la Rose* and before Jean de Meun's part appeared. The author was a certain Thibaut, who identifies himself anagrammatically in the poem, in this providing a precedent for later poets.[2] The prologue of the *Poire*, discussed in Chapter I in connection with indirect introductions similar to those of the *Duchess*, consists of several brief stories involving Cligés, Tristan, Piramus, and others. Following the prologue, the poet addresses his lady rhetorically (ll. 241-403), asking her mercy and protesting that he does not want to fight against Amor.

Throughout the rest of this 3027-line poem the narrator's speeches are continually interrupted by an unidentified interlocutor who skeptically asks him for explanations of his various

50

statements. The narrative proper begins (l. 404) with two allegorical representations of the process of falling in love. In the first, the poet tells how under a pear tree one day he shared a pear with his lady, and how this caused him to love her irrevocably. The interlocutor forces him to justify at length his statement that the resultant love was most sweet and most bitter. Elaborating, the poet discusses the power of love, citing the Piramus and Thisbe story and his authority, the *Metamorphoses*, Book IV.

> N'est pas mençonge, ainz est fins voirs
> A tesmoig d'Ovide, .I. preudome,
> El quart livre de la grant somme.   (ll. 735-737)

Another metaphor is now used (l. 770) to represent again the progress of this love affair from its beginning. The narrator states that he was besieged in the Tower of Pride by Biauté, Cortoisie, Noblece, and Franchise, the last of whom tells the lover a bit of the story of Paris and Helen to exemplify once more the power of Amor. Having been thus introduced, Amor appears and approaches the tower, attended by the song of many different kinds of birds and the music of many minstrels; he demands and receives the lover's fealty and, literally, his heart. Amor, who is said to be more beautiful than Absalom or Abel (ll. 1171-72), explains that he takes the lover's heart to keep him from being a traitor like Ganelon. With the heart in hand, Amor goes off to the city of Paris, which the poet praises for fifty lines (ll. 1324-78) as the location of the Court of Love and the home of the most beautiful ladies.

In the long remainder of the poem (ll. 1379-3027) the narrative involves Amor's choosing a lady for the lover, an exchange of hearts, a lengthy description of the lady's facial beauty (ll. 1615-1786), and complaints by the lover concerning his inferior station as compared with that of the lady and his fears of approaching the lady. In the course of these complaints Raison appears abruptly and advises the lover to give her up and choose someone from among his peers, but (as in *Roman de la Rose*) this advice is

51

disdained. The lady's and the poet's names (*Anne* and *Tibaut*) are revealed in an anagram, and the lady by a clever manipulation of the lover's name lets him know that she would be his: *Tua sit* (*Tibaut* spelled backwards with the *b* transmuted). As the poem ends the lovers are in accord, but are separated by a jealous husband. The lover gives his lady a nightingale as a token, and wishes aloud that the husband were a cuckold ("Car fust il cous," l. 2903); he curses *le jalous*:

> He, envieus, chose dolente,
> Que te vaut d'un amant grever?
> Par foi, por ce porras crever. (ll. 3015-17)

And he taunts him that their love will be immortalized by his *Romanz de la Poire*.[3]

Thus the narrative progresses from the symbolic eating of the pear (perhaps comparable to the love potion of Tristan, and certainly related to the eating of the apple in Genesis) to allegories involving a Tower of Pride, an exchange of hearts, and a lecture of Reason—and finally to some realistic taunting of the husband. The narrative ends approximately where Guillaume de Lorris' poem concludes, with the lovers hopelessly separated; this is simply one of the numerous parallels to the *Rose*.

Aside from the lover's undissembled desire to cuckold the husband (characteristic of the earlier *dits amoreux*), of particular interest to this study are the comparatively numerous literary allusions in the *Poire*. Thibaut cites Plato by name, and he narrates or alludes to stories of the *Metamorphoses* (Piramus and the Judgment of Paris), Chrétien's *Cligés*, some version of the Tristan legend, *Roland*, and the Bible. This small library is comparable to that which Guillaume de Lorris had utilized. Jean de Meun, writing after the *Poire*, in addition to Ovid parades the works and names of many classical authors: Cicero, Sallust, Vergil, Horace, Livy, Lucan, Suetonius, and Juvenal. He also employs material drawn from numerous medieval narratives and dissertations.[4] But the practice of allusion established in both

52

parts of the *Rose* and in the *Poire* seems to have exercised little influence on the writers of the *dits amoreux* after Jean de Meun up to the time of Machaut.

The frequency of literary allusion in the *dits* probably reflected the poet's social status, since a man of high social rank would generally have a better education and have more access to books. Thibaut's statements about his lady and his discussion of the city of Paris seem to confirm that he was a man of the upper classes. Likewise Machaut and Froissart, who evidenced considerable learning in their works, held important court positions. But the poets between Thibaut and Machaut were mostly simple *trouvères* who were no doubt ranked among the menials of the courts which they frequented. Their reading was evidently very narrow. Thus literary allusions in Jean de Condé's and Watriquet's poems are sparse and evidence no direct familiarity with the works referred to, and in works of other poets of this class literary reference is non-existent. This is the case with the next two poems to be considered here, the closely-related *Fablel dou Dieu d'Amours* and *De Venus la Deese d'Amor*.

In these two poems an allegorical love story frames a scenic description of the Palace of Love. Therefore they partake of both classes of episodic *dits* which I have posited, with the beginning and end of each forming a developed love narrative and the middle part consisting of scenes held together by a perambulatory observer. However, the importance of the love stories in these poems, which particularly in *De Venus* is overriding, justifies treating them at this point.

The poet of the *Fablel*[5] seems clearly to belong to the lower classes. His request for a drink in the middle of the poem[6] suggests that it was designed for tavern presentation, and the outcome of the birds' debate indicates that the poet was partial to the *vilains*. The poem as a whole, moreover, as its most recent editor observes, seems a mere compilation which a simple *jongleur* might have produced.[7]

Whatever the status of the poet and however disjointed the narrative, the poem is quite lively. The poet relates that one morning while he is lying in bed he dreams that he gets up to the song of the birds in Maytime, enters a meadow where every possible herb and flower is blooming, and walks along a stream which has youth-endowing qualities till he comes to a *vergier* enclosed by a moat paved with marble and surrounded by walls of carved ivory. The golden drawbridge, supported by pillars of black marble, raises itself automatically against the rude and dishonorable, but it allows the narrator to enter with no trouble. Once inside (strophe 18) he sits under a heavily-laden branch and thinks himself in Paradise. Above him the birds, summoned by the nightingale, have a debate. The falcon blames the deterioration of the practice of Amour on the low-born and asserts that only knights and clerks should be allowed to love. The thrush and jay disagree, believing that loving of itself confers knighthood and learning. If a man loves well and is well-loved, says the jay,

> Preus est et sages comme clers escolés,
> Et chevalier d'amors est adoubés.   (strophe 31, c-d)

The nightingale renders a verdict consonant with this opinion, stating that everyone who strives to love becomes *cortois*. The birds then departing, the narrator has a second dream.

He dreams that his *amie* comes to him and that he kisses her a hundred times. She is worried because they are alone and admonishes him to guard her honor. She confesses that she came there by strongly wishing it, then worries that she has been foolish to tell him so. Suddenly a great dragon appears and carries her away wailing. In answer to the lover's complaint the God of Love rides up, gives the narrator a lift to his castle, and rides off to recover the *amie*. The god's dress and his castle are made of allegorized materials: his belt of the green days in May, his collar of the loud song of a bird, the bridge to the castle of *dits* and *chansons*. The moat of sighs is running with lovers' tears, and the twelve pillars of the palace inside are formed by the months. A phoenix guarding the palace portal propounds a riddle (strophe 74),[8] which the dreamer must answer to be admitted. But he has no trouble identifying the phoenix itself as the one who is born without father or mother. Inside the castle many young men and women are playing chess and tables; they all stop to greet him. He tells his troubles and sings a *chanson* in praise of the beloved.

In the concluding strophes of the work (104-142) a young lady who lives in the palace shows the lover the God of Love's bedchamber and the tomb of her *ami*. He was the son of a king, she explains, whom she ran away with to marry. They were stopped in their flight by a proud knight, and both the lover and the meddling knight were killed in the duel which ensued. The God of Love then took her into his castle. While the young lady and the dreamer are returning to the castle, the God of Love reappears bringing the *amie* back. The god says that he has rescued her because of the lover's seven years of faithful service. The dreamer is so excited that he wakes up, and then is very upset to find that the *songe* has lied to him.

De Venus la Deese d'Amor, dating from the end of the thirteenth century, is written in the same monorime stanzas as the *Fablel*; it takes over from that poem fifty-two quatrains completely and twelve in part.[9] However, *De Venus* is over twice as long as the *Fablel*, running to 315 quatrains. Notable sections which have no counterpart in the *Fablel* are a long complaint by the lover and a lengthy dialogue between him and Venus. *De Venus* differs from other *dits amoreux* in being narrated in the third person.

At the beginning the poet proposes to tell the great troubles of a lover. This lover, he narrates, after a sleepless night goes walking in a *vergier* identical with that of the *Fablel*. Sitting under the same tree, the Amant hears the same discussion by the birds. Afterwards—the poem here diverging from the *Fablel*—the nightingale remains till the lover scares him away with a complaint which lasts for the next 336 lines (strophes 31-114). He laments that he has no sword to kill himself. Rather than Florie, his lady should be named Tristouse; and he should be called Morant rather than Amant. Love, he wails, is the opposite of childbirth: while the mother carries the child she is in pain, but then she forgets the pain after birth; on the other hand, it is sweet to carry a love affair, but most bitter when love is dislodged from the heart. Groaning, sighing, ears ringing, he passes out. The poet comments that "Morant" has a living death.

The lover reviving, Venus rides up on a mule accompanied by three *puceles* and three thousand birds who join in asking her to help this *vrais amans*. Venus tests the lover by asking if he wants to be cured of the love which is ruining his life. He vehemently answers *no*, then goes on to describe the lady, her physical beauty, her gentle heart, her understanding, and her humility and courtesy. Such perfection makes him confident that she will some day ease his sufferings. Venus agrees (strophe 167) that there must be pity in such a gentle lady. She compares Amans to the falcon who sets his eye on a certain bird and disdains five hundred others in favor of the one he is pursuing. When Venus promises her intercession with the God of Love, they all ride off to the Court of Love. There (strophe 235) they find the god on a bed of flowers; he embraces Venus with great affection. In contrast to the allegorized furnishings and materials of the *Fablel*, the chamber and its decorations here are composed of crystal, amber, and cut coral. However, the same maiden as in the earlier poem shows Amans the God of Love's chamber and the tomb of her beloved. In addition, he sees the embalming, funeral, and entombment of a true lover. The liver, lungs, heart, and kidneys of this loyal subject are removed and washed with white and red wine. The body is then dressed in fine garments, transported in a chariot of gold, and placed in a marvellously fine tomb.

By these sights Amans is reinforced in his desire to die in the service of the God of Love. The god holds court and has the nightingale make a *chartre* for the lover commanding the lady to love him loyally or else incur the god's displeasure. Amans rides back home where he is sleepless all night in expectation of seeing the lady. When he encounters her next day she willingly agrees to follow the God of Love's orders. The closing strophes are interesting for their mixing of sensuality with a prayer for lovers to Jesus Christ:

"Certes," dist ele, "dous amis, ci vos otroi m'amor,
Volentiers querrai medichine por oster vo dolor."
Entre ses bras l'acole estroit par grant dolchor,
Et dist: "Tors iors vos amerai loialment par amor."

Ensi furent li amant en ioie tot lor vie.
Or prions a Ihesu Crist, le fils (de) sainte Marie,
Que il conforte tos amans qui d'amor sont cargie,
Et confonde tos orgoillous, ou point n'a de pitie.

(strophes 314-315)

The lover's ultimate success in *De Venus* contrasts with his frustration at the end of the *Fablel*. Another difference between the two poems is the fact that *De Venus* has no dream frame, but this whole study should prove that the dream is not a crucial element in the tradition.[10] More significant is the addition of speeches and discussions in *De Venus*, which results in the emphasis in that poem being shifted away from the scenes and events toward monologue and dialogue. Precedents for such non-narrative sections are found in the long lectures of the God of Love and Raison in the *Roman de la Rose*, where Guillaume de Lorris manages to avoid the dull rhetoric in which his successors sometimes became bogged down.

As the allegorical aspect of the *dits amoreux* became less complex—as in the poems studied in this chapter—rhetoric and ornament came to dominate many of them. One type of rhetorical ornament which became particularly popular is the elaborate lover's complaint, such as is found in *Poire* (ll. 1852-2015) and *De Venus*. The *Rose* has two relatively brief lover's complaints (ll. 3782-96, 2449-2504) which supplied a model for the later more extended laments. As will be discussed in more detail later, in the fourteenth century complaints were often embodied in distinct lyric set-pieces. Guillaume de Machaut fixed on a special sixteen-line strophic form for the lengthy complaints of *Remede de Fortune* and the *Fonteinne amoreuse*; Froissart utilized the same form in the *Paradys d'Amours* and *Espinette amoreuse*. The "maner song" which the Black Knight utters in the *Book of the Duchess* is actually a complaint possessing its own rhyme scheme; furthermore, a great part of the knight's early monologue is essentially a complaint (ll. 560-709).

Besides complaints, intercalated set-pieces of many kinds came to be important ornaments in some of the *dits*, as is well-illustrated in the next of the episodic narrative so be considered here, Nicole de Margival's *Dit de la Panthère d'Amours*,[11] which is probably a source for Chaucer's *House of Fame*. Nothing is known of Nicole except that in addition to this 2665-line work he wrote a short poem on the vices and virtues. The *Panthère* contains not only numerous individual set-pieces by its author, but also several by other poets: Adam de le Halle, Drouart la Vache, and an otherwise unknown author referred to as Jean l'Épicier. In part as a result of the borrowings from Drouart, the composition of the *Panthère* is fixed between 1290 and 1328, most probably around the turn of the century.

In the forty-line introduction the poet declares that he writes this poem for his lady but does not dare send it to her; therefore he will give it to her friends to read in the hope that they will pass it on. Asleep at Soissons one Assumption Eve, he relates, in his dream he is carried by birds into a forest full of animals of all colors: lions, leopards, wild boars, bears, unicorns, deer, and numerous others. In a valley closed off by thorns and briars he sees another beast, colored with every hue, whom all the animals love for its sweet breath—except the dragon, who would be killed by the breath, since the dragon is so full of venom that he cannot stand the smell of anything pure.

The animals having left (l. 144), the dreamer hears many

58

musical instruments and sees a great crowd approaching, led by the God of Love, who is richly apparelled and wearing a crown. Pleading timidity, the narrator forthwith excuses himself for not having previously entered into the service of one of Love's *dames* or *damoiselles*, and he requests that the god interpret his vision of the multi-colored animal. The god explains that the panther (for thus is the animal to be identified) represents the dreamer's beloved, the colors her virtues, the sweet breath her words. The dragon is the covetous and envious enemy of love; the nettles, thorns, and brambles signify respectively amorous thoughts, desire, and slander. The low valley signifies the lady's humility and simplicity.

His lesson ended, the God of Love now proclaims (ll. 683-684) that all should disport themselves. The dreamer's horse suddenly jumps the hedge and carries him to where the panther is sleeping. He looks at her for a long time, but does not dare say anything (like Perceval in the Grail castle); at length he leaves, but he is badly wounded and thrown from his horse going back through the hedge. The God of Love assures him he would have gotten no worse wound had he spoken to the beloved panther, and he sends him to the Castle of Love with Esperance, Dous Penser, and Dous Souvenir to recuperate from his injuries. At the castle the convalescent lover recites a 142-line prayer (ll. 825-966), in decasyllabic couplets, that the God of Love will somehow let his lady know his love.[12] As if in answer the god and his wife Venus come to comfort the dreamer (ll. 979 ff.). The god advises the dreamer that he can find all the *science* of love in the "rommant de la Rose," and Venus tells him that he is cowardly; he responds that Paour has made him listen to her clerk Adam [de le Halle], and he recites three short lyrics of Adam's which advise suffering in silence. The goddess, persisting, gives the dreamer a sixty-line stanzaic *dit* to pass on to his lady along with a ring. She explains the meaning of the ring in a short lyric. He, however, has a dream within his dream in which the lady angrily rejects the poem and the ring; this vision makes him unable to follow the

59

goddess' instructions. To brace him up she quotes two poems of Adam's, and the God of Love cites the advice of Drouart la Vache, but the dreamer still has no courage and no friend he trusts. Then, responds the god, he must rely on Fortune.

In the company of Esperance, Dous Penser, and Dous Souvenir, the lover sets off for the castle of Fortune (ll. 1952 ff.), which he finds built on ice, half beautiful and half in ruins. Fortune at first assigns the newcomers to the wasted side of the castle, known as Adversité, which is in charge of Meseürs (Unhappiness). They suffer there a long time till Grace and Bone Volonté help them move to the other side, Prosperité, which is under the aegis of Eürs. There the panther lives. The dreamer, encouraged by Esperance, beseeches Grace to intercede for him. All join in urging the panther to be merciful, to which the panther accedes since her mother, Pitié, wishes it. The dreamer is in bliss till morning, when the guard signals day on his horn and wakens him.

In the final five hundred lines (2190-2665), after stating that everything in the dream was true except for his obtaining *merci*, the poet includes several short lyrics which protest his affection and express fear that his lady might accept another lover. Then he resolves to go to her with a *roundel* which tells his love, imagines her answering favorably in another, and quotes his happy answer in a third. Having pleaded for mercy once more, the poet states humbly that he is not very wise and is unaccustomed to rhyming about such big subjects. He hopes that all those who find errors will correct them without blaming him. Finally, he puts his name into an anagram, "Digne amour li cela" (l. 2652).

In the most recent comparison of the *House of Fame* with Nicole's poem, Albert C. Baugh finds the evidence of Chaucer's use of the *Panthère* inconclusive, stating that only one similarity in detail between the two works is not a matter of convention— the fact that Fortune's castle in the *Panthère* and Chaucer's House of Fame are built on foundations of ice.[13] It is not convenient at this point to discuss the various similarities of detail which were previously cited by Sypherd,[14] nor to bring forward others. For present purposes a brief inspection of structural affinities between Nicole's poem and the *House of Fame* will suffice.

The *House of Fame* has three books, each of which contains a separate episode: Geffrey's tour of the Palace of Venus, his instruction by the eagle, and his visit to the House of Fame. The *Panthère* may likewise be divided into the poet's visit to the valley, his instruction by Venus and the God of Love, and his experiences in the Castle of Fortune. Various edifices, it may be seen, are important sites of the action in the two works: in Chaucer's poem the Palace of Venus and the Houses of Fame and Rumour, and in Nicole's the Castles of Love and Fortune. Both poems, then, are episodic, with the episodes having a comparable nature, being presented in a similar pattern, and taking place in comparable locations. And they end at the homes of closely related personifications, Fame and Fortune, in each of which are people "dyversly served" (*HF*, 1. 1549). Chaucer makes explicit the affinity of Fame and Fortune, stating that Fame treats people without discrimination,

Ryght as her suster, dame Fortune,
Ys wont to serven in comune. (ll. 1547-48)

Certainly these similarities do not provide proof of a direct relationship between the English and the French works, but they do indicate a family resemblance. One substantial difference between the poems is found in the role of the narrator. In the *Panthère*, as in the *Fablel* and the *Poire*, the main action is provided by the love affair of the narrator.[15] In the *House of Fame*, on the other hand, as in the *Duchess* and the *Parliament of Fowls*, the narrator is primarily a passive reader, spectator, and listener. In this respect these works of Chaucer are more closely related to the second kind of episodic narrative to be dealt with

61

in this chapter. These are represented by two *dits* of Watriquet de Couvin and one of Jean de Condé.

Of Watriquet de Couvin next to nothing is known outside of what he reported of himself. The dateable poems among the thirty-two of his extant works were written between 1319 and 1329, which makes his apparent poetic demise coincide more or less with the beginning of Machaut's writing career. Couvin is a village in Hainault, the same northern province from which emerged Edward III's wife Philippa, Jean Froissart, and perhaps Chaucer's wife. But Watriquet, who identifies himself as poet to the Count of Blois and Gauchier de Châtillon,[16] obviously practiced his art farther to the south. Unlike Machaut, Froissart, and Chaucer, who filled important court and government positions, Watriquet was simply a court minstrel. As he himself states, he has no other skill than writing and reciting good poetry, and claims no other title than Lord of Pretty Verse.[17] Though his pretty verse is often merely versified preaching, the number of manuscript collections of it extant indicate that it was moderately popular.[18] The *dit amoreux* was not Watriquet's specialty, and the first poem of his to be considered here, the *Tournois des dames*, does not really merit the adjective *amoreux*. It is included, however, because it is closely allied to the love *dits* and is relevant to this study in other ways.

The 1276-line narrative of the *Tournois* is made up of an 119-line introduction and a series of five allegorical tableaux. In the middle of October 1327, the poet recounts, he is visiting and reciting before the Count of Blois at Montferrant, an estate of the Count. The countryside is alive, the woods full of game and resounding with the songs of many birds, whose names, calls, and imaginary conversations the narrator recites. It is such a beautiful time that the poet is happy as a fox in his den. One day after dinner he climbs up in a little tower where painted windows depict a tournament of ladies battling with mounted knights. The ladies are winning, either leading the knights off to prison or killing them. The poet cannot comprehend how weak women can

62

conquer the knights; he thinks so much about it that he is seized by a vision. A female figure appears and asks why the poet is lying there, neither awake nor asleep. He replies that he is dazed from trying to understand the meaning of the painted glass, and he asks her name. She says that she is Verité, and that the tournament represents the battle of the soul with the body, showing how the stronger soul lets itself be subjugated.

Promising to show him many more wonderful visions, Verité leads him from the castle into a broad highway. The first thing they see is a stone bridge, beautiful but with rotten supports, from which people are falling in great numbers. Though the others on the bridge are paying no attention, the poet recoils, shouting *harou*. Verité explains that the bridge is the world and the black river beneath is hell. The next notable sight is two piles of carrion, one made up of fat horses, cattle, and swine, and the other consisting of scrawny little lambs and piglets. The dogs and birds that feed on the large pile are very thin, but those nourishing themselves on the small pile are prospering. Verité explains that those eating the fat carrion are the avaricious whose hunger for the goods of this world is never satisfied. The others are those who think only of serving God; they never want. The text concludes with two additional allegorized tableaux, one involving a lamb who conquers a lion, and the other a flooding river, which represents the ravages of a tyrant. Verité promises to show additional sights, but the poem breaks off at this point.

One detail in the *Duchess* suggests that Chaucer may have known Watriquet's *Tournois*. After the dreamer in the *Duchess* awakens in his dream to the song of birds, he looks around and sees that his room is decorated, walls and windows, with the stories of Troy and the *Roman de la Rose*. There are numerous precedents in literature for surfaces being used to depict stories: the *Aeneid*, Marie de France's *Guigemar*, the first terrace of Dante's *Purgatory*, and many others. The personifications portrayed on the wall of the garden in the *Rose* also provide an analoque. None of these, however, is as directly suggestive of

63

Chaucer's scene as the windows painted and inscribed with the
Tournament of Ladies in Watriquet's work:

> En un tornelle petite,
> De verrieres painte et escripte,
> Belle et gente et de riche atour;
> Si vi .i. tournoi tout entour
> Pourtrait et paint en la verriere,
> Dont j'oi merveille moult très fière.　　　　　(ll. 123-128)

As with the *Duchess* the painted windows in the *Tournois* are
connected with the beginning of the vision. In addition, both
poems state that there is writing along with the pictures in the
windows; and Veritez' statement that she has shown the poet
"la verité toute et la glose" (l. 459) of the depicted story is
suggestive of the language of the *Duchess*, where the windows are
said to have both "text and glose" of the *Romance of the Rose*.

The second poem of Watriquet's to be considered is his only
genuine *dit amoreux*, the *Dis de la Fontaine d'Amours*. Of
uncertain date, this 330-line work has a number of similarities to
Machaut's *Dit de la Fonteinne amoreuse*. In the middle of both
poems there is a dream inspired by the Fountain of Love which
has waters of magical powers in love, and in both cases the dream
takes up only about a third of the total poem. Watriquet's story
begins one morning in May with the poet's entering a garden
whose gate is standing open. The perfume of the flowers and the
song of the birds delight him. Proceeding into the garden he
finds a beautiful fountain inlaid with precious stones, which
Venus has appointed Celer, Loiauté, and Sens to guard. The
fountain has three inexhaustible basins: Jonesce, Prouesce, and
Largesse.

Pensers and Desirriers encourage the narrator to drink so much
from the fountain that he becomes thoroughly intoxicated and is
stretched out on the ground. Venus sends Espoirs and Souvenir
to his aid, but the poet only partially recovers and laments his
love-sickness till he falls asleep. In his dream the messenger of

64

Venus commands him to go to the Court of Love. Obeying, he travels through many a realm, duchy, and county before he arrives at his destination. He is just in time for dinner, at which are served successive courses of looks, sighs, complaints, *dangier*, and tarts made up of the flour of Jalousie, basted with tears, adorned with melancholy, and cooked in deep thoughts with amorous desire. The poet wakes up spontaneously after this repast, and the poem ends abruptly.

The narrator in the *Fontaine* participates in the allegorical episodes, as he does not in the *Tournois*, but his participation is incidental to the narrative, and there is no specific love affair involved in the action. The interest here, as in the first part of the *Roman de la Rose*, is centered on what is seen. Very much like the *Fontaine* in mode is Jean de Condé's *Messe des oisiaus et plais des chanonesses et des grises nonains*, which has a love-meal that is obviously related to Watriquet's work.

Jean's editor[19] surmises from the dateable poems that he lived from about 1280 to 1345. He belonged to the household of Guillaume de Hainault and also travelled about France and Flanders. Charles-Victor Langlois notes that Jean resembles Watriquet "like a brother. Of the same country, the same profession, contemporaries, disciples and representatives of the same tradition, the major part of the literary baggage of these two men is almost interchangeable."[20] There is no known record of Jean de Condé outside his works, which exist in four manuscripts.[21]

The events of the 1580-line *Messe des oisiaus* are all contained in a dream. The poet, while thinking of the joys of lovers, falls asleep contentedly one night and dreams that he is in a lovely forest on a knoll, under a large branchy tree. An innumerable throng of birds congregates around him, and a parrot announces the approach of Venus. Her coming is accompanied by a serenade of all the birds. The sun having just risen, Venus proclaims that she will hold court only after they have heard Mass and dined.

Venus orders the nightingale to have Mass sung (ll. 113-370). The nightingale chants the Confiteor, the larks begin the Introit, and all the birds join in to finish it and sing the Kyrie. They also accompany the nightingale in the Gloria, during which the cuckoo is chased away for his discordant croaking. The mavis reads the Epistle, the merlin the Gospel, and Venus orders the parrot to preach the sermon. His theme is that he who hopes for joy in love needs four virtues: obedience, patience, loyalty, and hope. In closing he enjoins all true lovers to pray their ladies' pardon for their misdeeds in "penser, œvre, et parler." After the sermon, the cuckoo revenges himself by screaming "tout cuku," and hides in a hole of a tree. The service continues. Instead of a host a red rose is elevated, from which the priest (the nightingale is never explicitly equated with the priest) takes three petals, but the rose remains whole. After the Mass the birds ask that Venus allow them to punish the cuckoo, but Venus tells them to ignore that bad bird which eats its mother, for, as one often hears said, "The more dung is stirred, the more it smells."

The serving of dinner, in which people rather than birds participate, now provides another lengthy ritual (ll. 417-646). Laity and clerics, maidens and wives are present. The first course is of looks, some of which the poet steals, but he is unable to get any of the sweet smiles that are passed out next. Desire, however, is a very generous wine-steward, and the poet and many others become drunk, but this is no disgrace at Venus' court. There is an entrecourse of sighs and complaints, and some diners are then served roasted derision with jealousy sauce, but the poet refuses this overcooked dish. The poet asks one lady with a platter full of fair answers and sweet grantings for some of her dish, but she gives him only of the former. The servants bring to the ladies dishes of hugs and kisses; the poet angers one lady by asking for a kiss, but at least he manages to steal a hug. The meal over, the covers are removed and a minstrel plays an *estampie* on the *vielle* while many others also ply their minstrelsy.

Now Venus holds court for all those who have requests or complaints (ll. 647-1218). A canoness of great nobility speaks first. She complains that the gray nuns with their easy virtue are stealing the canonesses' knightly lovers from them. A gray nun responds that her convent has ladies who are as young, pretty, and amorous as any. The canoness rejoins that her order has served Love longer than the nuns, and she demands that they take their monks and abbotts and leave the gentlemen alone, to which the gray nun retorts that a poor lady can be as good to love as a noblewoman. The argument having disintegrated into a quarrel, Venus interrupts to pronounce judgment. The goddess states that she has power, after God and Nature, over all creatures, that she receives Jew, Christian, and Saracen, young and old, rich and poor. She prizes the canonesses for their long service, but it would be contrary to Nature to banish the nuns from her court. She concludes with an injunction to both groups to continue their faithful service.

Jean spends the long remainder of the poem (ll. 1219-1580) in moralizing his narrative. The meanings of the funny stories which he has told, he states, are quite disguised; they have a divine application (*diviniteis*), though they seem vain. He will explain part, though it would be too much to gloss all. The cuckoo represents those who do wrong against the Church and also slanderers. The rose is a worthy representative of the host. The canonesses' complaint against the parvenu gray nuns is comparable to the complaint of the workers in the vineyard who went out early, but were paid the same as those who went out late. He has hidden morality in this way, Jean explains, so that he may please both the wise and the fools—the wise may take example and the fools will be solaced by the humor. In closing he adds that both the canonesses and gray nuns do wrong in loving outside marriage, for all who enter into religious lives should put their hearts wholly on God (The dream is not explicitly ended).

In the first part of the *Roman de la Rose*, the prototype for the three works just taken up, what the narrator sees prepares him for what subsequently happens to him. But in the works where observation is the narrator's primary role throughout, as in those of Watriquet and Jean de Condé and in Chaucer's dream poems, his presence needs to be justified by some other motivation. Jean and Watriquet did not always supply this. In the *Messe des oisiaus*, the Mass and the meal are represented as requisite preliminaries to Venus' holding court, but these three major incidents of the poem have no organic relationship to each other beyond the fact that love is the subject of all three. As with Watriquet's *Fontaine*, the narrator as spectator serves as a linking character, but in neither poem is he given explicit motivation for being there. Deprived of an active role as a lover, he seems an idle sightseer. In Watriquet's *Tournois*, however, Veritez' anxiety to instruct the narrator gives more point to his presence, and in another of Watriquet's works, the *Mireoirs as dames*,[22] the narrator's participation is more specifically justified by his guide's interest in supplying him material for a "biau dit". Similarly, the eagle in the *House of Fame* takes Geffrey on a trip to give him tidings of fame, and the dreamer at the end of the *Duchess* thinks of his experience as having furnished him material for a poem:

> Thoghte I, "Thys ys so queynt a sweven
> That I wol, be processe of tyme,
> Fonde to put this sweven in ryme."   (ll. 1330-32)

Not only does Chaucer in his dream poems provide a better rational basis for the presence of his narrator than Watriquet and Jean generally provide in their *dits*, but also he gives his poems a logical development which their works lack. Yet these early works of Chaucer, because they consist of a series of observed scenes which lack a narrative connection, rather resemble the first part of the *Rose* and this later type of episodic poem than the *dits* which are composed of centralized allegories or of episodes connected by narrative development. There is on the other hand a sense in which neither the *Rose* nor any of the *dits* studied to this point offer a precedent to the *Duchess*, since the main episode in Chaucer's poem is a developed narrative in which no personification participates actively and there is no ostensible psychological or moral allegory. It remained for the French poets who follow those studied thus far—Guillaume de Machaut and Jean Froissart—to provide the model for this kind of story. The works of these two poets and their influence on Chaucer will be the subject of the next four chapters.

The *dits* which have been the subject of the last two chapters exercised their main influence on Chaucer indirectly through Machaut and Froissart. It would not, however, be proper to conclude that Chaucer was unfamiliar with the earlier *dits* at first hand and was not directly influenced by them. Historical circumstance and his poetry itself suggest that he read or heard read a substantial number of them; certainly, his poetry provides no reason for thinking that he disdained them.

CHAPTER IV

GUILLAUME DE MACHAUT

French poets imitated Guillaume de Lorris' *Roman de la Rose* for a hundred years after its composition without achieving any substantial uniformity of mode in their love narratives. Finding the whole of Guillaume's model inimitable, they experimented with copying its various parts. But their experiments were not in turn imitated. It remained for Guillaume de Machaut to develop from the *Rose* and its progeny a mode which other poets could and did utilize. Poets in France, most notably Froissart, Christine de Pisan, and Alain Chartier used Machaut's works as models in the composition of their *dits*, and so also did Geoffrey Chaucer in his first long poem, the *Book of the Duchess*. Though the prologue of the *Duchess* is for the most part related in structure and detail to works other than Machaut's, every facet of the elegy proper—mode, form, and detail—is permeated with the influence of Machaut's *dits*. The connection is so strong as to make it remarkable that Chaucer's originality shows through as it does.

This chapter is devoted to supplying general background information about Machaut, to considering several of his long narratives, and to showing some of the minor connections of his work with Chaucer's, this all being prefatory to a consideration in the following two chapters of his four most important and influential *dits*.

Like Chaucer, Guillaume de Machaut, though not of the

nobility, was a close associate of some of the leading court figures of his time. Again like Chaucer he made himself valuable to his patrons in ways other than through his poetry, so that his social status was considerably higher than that historically enjoyed by the *trouvère* of common birth. Unlike Chaucer, he was a cleric. Nothing is known of his education beyond the fact that he became a priest. He derived his surname from the village of Machaut in the district of the Ardennes where he was born about 1300.[1] Around 1323 he entered the service of Jean of Luxembourg, King of Bohemia, whom he served for years as chaplain and secretary, travelling with him throughout Europe. With the help of Jean, Guillaume became canon of Reims, and he evidently retired to this canonry prior to 1340, several years before the death of his adventuresome and generous royal patron in 1346. In 1349 Machaut in his debate poem, the *Jugement dou Roy de Navarre*, evidenced an association with another king, Charles le Mauvais of Navarre. Charles appears in that work as judge, just as Jean of Luxembourg had appeared in the earlier *Jugement dou Roy de Behaingne*. Machaut wrote another long poem, the *Confort d'Ami*, to console Charles in prison in 1357, but the two men evidently became estranged soon after that when Charles became an open enemy of the French monarchy. Machaut in the following years cultivated his relationships with Jean le Bon of France and his two sons, one of whom (the Duc de Berry) is the main character in the *Dit de la Fonteinne amoreuse*. In 1370 Machaut completed his last long poem, the *Prise d'Alexandrie*, celebrating the feats of Pierre de Lusignan, King of Cyprus. The poet died in 1377.

Eustache Deschamps, who referred to Chaucer as "grand translateur" in a famous *balade*, wrote two *balades* lamenting "la mort Machaut, la noble rethorique."[2] In another *balade* addressed to Peronne, who is probably the lady in question in Machaut's pseudo-autobiographical *Voir Dit*, Deschamps praises his fellow poet and admits a great personal indebtedness to him:

Machaut qui tant vous a amé
Et qui estoit la fleur de toutes flours,
Noble poëte et faiseur renommé,
Plus qu'Ovide vray remede d'amours,
Qui m'a nourry et fait maintes doucours.[3]

Though Machaut's greatest literary importance probably results from his influence on Chaucer, the intrinsic merit of his work largely supports Deschamps' encomium. His innovations were extensive and his applications of them often successful, so that a substantial part of his poetry, both of his lyrics and his longer *dits*, is original and has literary worth.

Much of the credit for establishing the fixed form of the lyric for the fourteenth and fifteenth centuries, as Hoepffner states, must go to Machaut:

> Il fait triompher, s'il ne les crée pas lui-même, les genres à formes fixes, la ballade, le chant royal, le virelai, le rondeau et le lai, qui, avec quelques variations et certaines modifications, règneront jusqu'au seiziéme siècle.[4]

Even if the value of these innovations is sometimes questionable, particularly in the premium which they place on complicated rhymes, the assessment of Alfred Jeanroy is certainly extreme. Jeanroy speaks of the banality, prolixity, and platitude of Machaut's lyrics, and describes them as spreading out in two enormous volumes in which one would have trouble finding twenty verses worth citing:

> Novateur, il le fut en effet; mais ses innovations ne portent que sur le vêtement de la poésie lyrique, sur ces deux accessoires qui alors étouffent l'essentiel, la musique et la versification.[5]

Chaucer, Froissart, and Deschamps, men with great claim to literary judgment, nevertheless followed Machaut's lyric forms, and each imitated the diction and content of considerably more than twenty lines of his short poems.

Machaut's lyrics are divided in manuscript on a varying principle, sometimes according to subject and sometimes according to form. The first division, entitled the *Louange des dames,* consists of 224 poems, a mixture of *balades* and *rondels* with several *chansons royals* and one *chanson baladée.* A second division contains 10 complaints, which are related in content but do not have a set form. Subsequent divisions, however, are composed of one type with quite strict form: 24 *lays;* 23 *motets;* and substantial individual sections of *ballades notées, chansons baladées,* and *rondeaux.* Most of these works are French, though some are Latin and French, and some Latin only.

Chaucer's short poems—complaints, balades, and roundels—certainly owe aspects of their form to Machaut's lyrics. In addition, the content of Chaucer's work is indebted to several of his lyrics, the *Duchess* reflecting details of at least four of them. Several lines of the Black Knight's complaint come from the complaint against Fortune in Machaut's Eighth Motet. The suggestion for the image of Fortune as a scorpion in the *Duchess* (ll. 636-641) seems to come from the Latin Ninth Motet. The *Lay de Confort* was no doubt the original for the Black Knight's declaration that all the planets in the sky make him weep (ll. 693-696), and also for his statement of the value of serving his lady "for noght" (ll. 844-845). Finally, the Thirty-Eighth Balade Notée probably helped supplement Chaucer's list of non-pareils (ll. 1054-71). Of course these borrowings are of minor importance in themselves, but the fact that they come from three distinct manuscript divisions is an interesting indication that Chaucer read through a substantial portion of the lyrics.[6]

Of more central concern in this study of the *dits amoreux* and Chaucer are the longer works of Machaut. Ten poems of his have over a thousand lines each. Of these, eight are *dits amoreux;* the *Confort d'Ami* is a poem of consolation and advice addressed to Charles of Navarre; and the *Prise d'Alexandrie* is a verse chronicle. These last two poems are interesting from the standpoint of contemporary history and provide important biographical information about Machaut, but they are not relevant here. Of the others, the eight *dits amoreux*, four are especially important as sources for Chaucer and the *Book of the Duchess*: the two judgment poems, of the Kings of Navarre and Behaingne; and two poems of complaint and comfort, the *Remede de Fortune* and the *Dit de la Fonteinne amoreuse*. They provide the subject matter for the following two chapters. The other four, taken up briefly in this chapter, are significant primarily for their place in and contributions to the French love-narrative tradition. These include the *Dit dou Vergier*, the earliest of Machaut's *dits amoreux*; the *Dit dou Lyon*; the *Dit de l'Alerion*; and the last of his love stories, the *Voir dit*.

The standard order of the Machaut manuscripts places his ten long poems at the beginning in approximately chronological order, preceded in several manuscripts by a Prologue.[7] In the Prologue a personified Nature presents to the poet three of her children, Scens, Retorike, and Musique, and the poet expresses his desire to write polite verse. He states that the poet who is attentive to these gifts of Nature is unable to think of anything evil,

Ou villenie fust enclose
Haïne, baras ou mesdis.   (V. 34-35)

Machaut's poetry generally lives up to this protestation of politeness in the Prologue. In none of his works is there bawdry, nor even any unequivocal references to the pleasures of the bed, except for short passages in the *Voir dit*, where the references are mitigated by the tone and brevity of the allusions. Thus his love narratives are generally applicable to all kinds of love situations, even to the purest, as the earlier *dits amoreux* often had not been.

The *Dit dou Vergier*, a 1293—line poem, follows the Prologue in the manuscripts. The vision frame of this thoroughly conventional narrative is of some interest because Machaut did not thereafter use visions to frame his stories. The narrator begins by telling of getting up from his bed in May and entering a *jardinet*. He

74

proceeds down a *sentelette*, enjoying the flowers and the melody of the birds, until he finds a *vergier*, a terrestrial paradise with one especially beautiful tree in the center. Sitting and thinking about his lady, the narrator becomes entranced. Amours then appears to him along with six young men and six young ladies. Perched in the tree, the god introduces the men as Voloir, Penser, Dous Plaisir, Loiauté, Celer, and Desir, and tells how, when a lover asks for "le don" (l. 787), they battle against Dangier, Paour, Honte, Durté, Cruauté, and Doubtance. If it were not for the young ladies here, he continues—Grace, Pitié, Esperance, Souvenir, Franchise, and Attemprance—the lover would be lost. These ladies, however, always vanquish the *villeins*, and Amours grants the lovers

> De la joie don et ottroy.
> Mais c'est toudis sauve l'onneur
> Des dames et sans deshonneur. (ll. 1052-54)

In answer to the narrator's request Amours promises to help him if he conducts himself properly. As the god leaves he shakes cold dew in the narrator's face, which wakes him up. He resolves to follow the god's directions and await the gift which has been promised him.

Though the substance of this poem is hackneyed, the work does show Machaut rejecting the episodic structure which characterized a substantial part of the *Roman de la Rose* and which many of its imitators had adopted. The *Dit dou Vergier* is unified in scene and action. Furthermore, allegory is found in it only on the level of dialogue, in Amour's description of the lover's struggle. The real action of the story, the visit of the God of Love and his court to a garden, is not basically allegorical. Machaut in this poem thus initiates a new kind of *dit amoreux*, one step farther away than its predecessors from the *Roman de la Rose*. The writers of the centralized allegories attained unity by rejecting the episodic first section of Guillaume de Lorris' work, but they retained the allegory. In the episodic narratives the role

75

and development of the allegory is reduced, but these poems lack unity. Guillaume de Machaut unifies the narrative and reduces or eliminates the allegory in the *Dit dou Vergier* and in most of his subsequent narratives. Chaucer takes over this unified, non-allegorical form for his elegy in the *Book of the Duchess*, though the prologue has the episodic beginning of the *Rose*.

Both de-emphasis of allegory and unity of action are features of the two judgment poems of Machaut which follow the *Dit dou Vergier* in most manuscripts. The plots are simple and coherent, each consisting of a debate section followed by a section in which a judgment is made. The following work, the *Remede de Fortune*, has a somewhat more complex, but still unified, plot line in which the lover's troubles are complicated and then resolved. The *Dit dou Lyon*, which generally appears fifth among Machaut's long poems, is more episodic than the others, since the series of experiences of the narrator leads to no particular conclusion. But the fact that these experiences all take place on a single small island and that they are held together by the figure of the lion gives the poem a coherence which the episodic *dits* described in the last chapter do not have. The *Dit dou Lyon* is of particular interest to the Chaucerian scholar as a possible prototype of Chaucer's lost "book of the Leoun," mentioned in his Retraction and by Lydgate; it is also a minor source for the *Book of the Duchess*.

In the first thirty lines the poet remarks that all creation, especially the birds, delights in spring. He goes on to tell how on April 3, 1342, he was awakened by birds, among them the calendar lark, who can predict the death or survival of a sick person by looking at him or away from him. He fancies that this lark is like his lady, who protects him when she looks at him. His train of thought having led him to the lady, he can sleep no more, so he walks to the river which runs near the manor he is visiting. Across the river is a *vergier* which contains all trees and flowers worth praising. Though there is no bridge to it, the narrator finds on the bank a beautiful boat which carries him across the river under its own power. When he walks into the lovely wood, a ferocious lion all at once rushes on him. But the lion suddenly becomes docile when the narrator commends his soul to his lady, crying, "Chiere dame, a vous me commant" (l. 313). Evidently wholly won over by this attestation of true love, the lion leads him by the shirttail through a wild place full of thorns and brambles, and dragons, serpents, scorpions, and all sorts of wild beasts, including one with two horns which is especially terrifying, whose species the narrator says he cannot identify [the *jaloux* as cuckold?]. These beasts nag at the lion but are afraid to attack him. Finally, the lion and the narrator come upon a fair meadow above a spring, where, in front of a tent, a most beautiful lady wearing a crown is sitting on an exquisite Carthaginian carpet, with many squires, knights, *dames*, and *damoiselles* around her.

The lion at this point (l. 499) begins frisking around and kneels before the lady, then goes up to her with his tail between his legs. The lady pats him, but when she is distracted by the great two-horned beast, the lion immediately becomes despondent. The puzzled narrator approaches and asks the lady to explain the boat, the river, and the wood. She calls on a wise and aged chevalier to answer him, and the ensuing disquisition of the old knight (ll. 853-1800), taking up almost half of the poem's 2204 lines, is the *pièce de résistance* of the work. He explains that all types of lovers used to come to this *vergier*, the false and the true: liars who took the ladies for fools, the properly humble, and false complainers who betrayed themselves by their failure to change color as true lovers do. May such be hung or flayed or eaten by dogs, exclaims the old knight. Also false warriors came, who liked to joust at home but did not go abroad as those do who fight for the honor of their ladies from Cyprus to Siloh right up to the Dry Tree. There were those who besieged the ladies indiscriminately and later bragged about their conquests. Finally, there were the clownish Robins, fed on milk and cheese, cabbage and turnips, who danced the *reverdie* with their loves, and could not do anything but snigger when the *bergères* spoke to them.

Among the women, on the other hand, were the flatterers and liars and those who came only to dance and play, as well as those who loved truly their fighters in far-off lands. There were the easily-won and the coquettes who covertly pinched the fingers and nudged the feet of admirers whom they had no intention of loving. Because so many traitors came there, an ancestor of the lady with the crown had the world's cleverest builders dig the river and make the magic boat, making it impossible for false lovers to gain entry. He named the place "L'Espreuve de fins amours." The old knight closes by enjoining the narrator to be loyal so that he will continue to be free to come and go.

The lady herself explains about the lion (ll. 1845-2074), who is upset by the nagging of the other beasts. She has fed and trained him since he was small, she says, and still gives him everything he eats. Thus she keeps him under control and from taking revenge on the other animals. The narrator protests that the lion suffers too much, but the lady responds that he will learn by suffering, it being proverbial that "He who suffers, conquers." The narrator's curiosity now satisfied, the lion leads him back to the boat, bowing to the narrator as he embarks to signal his thanks for the attempted help. When the narrator gets back to the manor he tells the assembled company of his experience. They all start to make plans to visit the *vergier*, but he wonders if they all will be able to. The poet then gives his name in an anagram and asks Amour to keep him from misdeeds. (ll. 2171-2204).

The list of points of chivalric wandering in the *Duchess* (ll. 1024-29) is partially indebted to the warriors' destinations named by the aged knight, as was mentioned in the last chapter. The possible relationship of the *Lyon* to Chaucer's lost *Book of the Leoun* is intriguing, but nearly useless to speculate about. A further relationship of this poem to Chaucer's works, which is more susceptible of discussion, is that of the lion-guide to the little dog of the *Duchess* and to other of Chaucer's guides.

As Africanus led Scipio on a tour of the spheres, as Vergil led

Dante through Hell and Purgatory, so (at least in a sense) the
puppy leads Chaucer's dreamer into the wonderful *destour*:

> I was go walked fro my tree,
> And as I wente, ther cam by mee
> A whelp, that fauned me as I stood,
> That hadde yfolowed, and koude no good.
> Hyt com and crepte to me as lowe
> Ryght as hyt hadde me yknowe,
> Helde down hys hed and joyned hys eres,
> And leyde al smothe doun hys heres.
> I wolde have kaught hyt, and anoon
> Hyt fledde, and was fro me goon;
> And I hym folwed... (ll. 387-397)

While this puppy is a descendant of the traditional guides of
older literature, his immediate parents are three Machaut animals,
the bird which the narrator follows in *Behaingne*, the dog in the
same poem, and the lion of the *Dit dou Lyon*. The bird of
Behaingne (ll. 25-32) is like the dog of the *Duchess* in that it leads
the narrator into the *destour* and then disappears from the poem.
The lady's *petit chien*, which runs up to the narrator and bites at
him, and is carried back by him to the lady (ll. 1202-13), provides
a counterpart to Chaucer's puppy in animal family, size, and
point of appearance in the poem. But it is the lion which has the
personality of Chaucer's little dog.

In the manner in which the lion approaches both the narrator
and the lady in the *Dit dou Lyon* there is a relationship to the
little dog's actions in the *Duchess*. In Chaucer's poem the dog
creeps up to the dreamer as if he knows him; he holds his head
down, joins his ears, and puts his hair down smooth. The lion
goes through a similar ritual when he catches sight of his mistress.
He rears back his head, pricks up his ears, wags his tail, and
paws the ground for joy (ll. 499-509). Then he goes up to her
with his tail between his legs. When previously the lion recognized
the narrator as a true lover, he was specifically compared to a
little dog; exactly like Chaucer's dog he joined his ears:

79

Lors vint vers moy tout belement
Li lions, *aussi humblement*
Com se fust un petit chiennet.
Et quant ce vi, je dis: "Bien est."
Si li mis ma main sur la teste,
Mais plus doucement qu'autre beste
Le souffri et *joint les oreilles*.   (ll. 325-331)

Machaut's lion and Chaucer's dog, then, act in similar ways; but both the bird and dog of *Behaingne* must also be counted among the direct antecedents of Chaucer's guide.

Much more completely than the dog, the lion represents the poetic guide of tradition: he leads with obvious understanding of what he is doing, and he protects his ward. One of the most common functions of the guide is as instructor. Thus Oiseuse in the *Rose* tells Amant all about the Garden of Deduit before leading him to the *carole*; Verité leads the narrator and instructs him with her parables in Watriquet's *Tournois des dames*; and in Froissart's *Paradys d'Amours* Experance and Plaisance are guides, instructors, and playmates for the narrator-lover. Compared to the generality of the guides of the *dits amoreux*, then, Chaucer's dog has quite a restricted function. In the *Parliament of Fowls*, too, Scipio has comparatively little prominence; he simply shows the narrator the garden gates and shoves him through. The eagle of the *House of Fame* does a more complete job of guiding, for he provides complete transportation and superabundant instruction. He is in fact a parody of the usual preachy and all-knowing guide. All three of these Chaucerian guides, it might be noted, provide light touches in their poems, as does the lion in his.

The two other *dits amoreux* of Machaut to be dealt with in this chapter contain a new kind of love story. In the traditional *dit* the allegorical framework and decorative appurtenances of the stories may vary, but the implicit narrative of love is much the same. The lovers all go through great sufferings to attain recognition from the lady whom they are fated to serve by the irrevocable decree of Amour. Under cover of the allegory of the *Dit de l'Alerion*, however, the lover deals with four different ladies, each of whom he philosophically gives up as necessity dictates, a procedure quite novel to the tradition. The *Voir Dit*, similarly unorthodox, is a long tale of an affair which the lady instigates and in which the lover is considerably less than dauntless. The expected conventional narratives in both cases have given way to stories which are non-conventional; presumably they are more realistic, perhaps being based, as they purport to be, on actual experiences of the poet.

The *Dit de l'Alerion* is the third longest[8] of Machaut's poems, and his least successful *dit*, perhaps because he attempts in this work to construct a centralized allegory when he nowhere displays any facility with allegory. The allegorical machinery in the *Alerion* in any event is presented awkwardly and is quite undeveloped; the poet's explanations of the allegory and his digressions seem interminable.

As a youth, the poet begins, he became fond of birds, so he learned from experienced people how to deal with them. One might thus learn about love, he asserts. So also might one choose a girl inexperienced in love as he himself chose to acquire an untrained *epervier* (sparrow-hawk) rather than a proven one or one in training. When he located a very attractive hawk after a long search and observed its habits closely, he set about capturing it with bait, just as a lover uses a "dous amoreus regart" and courteous speech to capture his prey. He trained and enjoyed his *épervier* over a long period of time, but then it had to moult, and when it came out of mew it was lost to him (l. 1259). Though disappointed, he reconciled himself and fell next in love with an *alerion* (an eagle, probably in this case a small one) which belonged to another; he longed for it so much that finally those in charge of the bird gave it to him, just as St. Louis gave his horse to Guillaume de Longue Espée. The *alerion*, however, eventually was lost (l. 2957). Bonne Amours consoled him by conferring on him an eagle of very high quality, but he lost it too in an unexplained manner. He also had to release the gerfalcon which he subsequently acquired and entertained himself with, for the gerfalcon one day left the pursuit of its proper prey to take up with a *chahuant*, "un oisel lait, vil et puant" (l. 4221). Thus are lovers sometimes treated by their ladies, he muses. To console himself for this final loss he went into an arbor, where Aventure, Fortune, and Nature combined to give him peace. For there the *alerion* whom he had loved returned to him; he recognized it by a jewel he had placed on its foot. The work ends with a comparison of this reunion with that of lovers, and with an acrostic identifying the poet.

Not only does the *Dit de l'Alerion* suffer from Machaut's failure to develop the allegorical frame of falconry which he adopts—as Jehan Acart, for example, developed the frame of the hunt in his *Prise amoreuse*—but also the very novelty of the narrative underlying the allegory detracts from the poem. Though originality is a great virtue in modern fictional modes, the same is not true in the fourteenth-century love story. The introduction of an individualized non-typical love narrative into a form composed mostly of conventional elements leaves the resulting work without a great part of the idealized, romantic quality that is perhaps the major aesthetic virtue of the *dit amoreux*.

In the narrative of the *Voir Dit*, likewise unconventional, Machaut insists on the truth of its every detail:

Le Voir-Dit vueil-je qu'on appelle
Ce traictié que je fais pour elle
Pour ce que ja n'i mentiray.   (ll. 430-432)

Further conducing to an effect of realism in the work is the relegation of allegory to the level of diction, this being in line with Machaut's usual practice but in contrast to the *Alerion*. The primary elements which remain to relate the *Voir Dit* to the tradition are its conventional expression, its numerous interspersed lyrics, and its frequent allusions and *exempla*, mostly classical. The resulting mixture of innovation with convention produces another mostly tedious work. With 9031 verses, including numerous intercalated rondels, virelays, and other set-pieces, along with 46 prose letters, it is by far Machaut's longest work, and it is the last of his *dits amoreux*, dating from 1363 or 1364.

The aging poet, publicizing his retained vigor, so clearly means the story to be taken as autobiography that there is little distortion in referring to the narrator as the *poet*. To begin the story he tells of receiving a rondel from a lady of quality in which she confesses an interest in him. He sends a rondel in return, thus initiating an exchange of love lyrics and letters which eventually leads to an eight-day visit by the poet to the lady's home. He receives her promise of mercy and leaves for home to make a novena, during which time she visits him, and they enjoy numerous kisses in the church. After returning home, she goes to Paris, and he visits her there. But the two are not alone till the day the lady is to leave, at which time the poet finally is received in her chamber, she with no other attire than "les uevres de nature" (l. 3692). In answer to the poet's prayer, Venus descends and covers the lovers with a cloud, and the lady entrusts to him "la clef de mon tresor" (l. 3891). Shortly after her departure, Desir starts bothering the poet, and he writes a complaint about it; the lady assures him by letter that no one will be around the next time they get together.

The next time, however, never comes, at least not in the poem. The lovers send many poems and letters back and forth, and she sends him love tokens in answer to his request. He dreams that she is wearing green, a sign that she has taken a new lover; she dreams that she heals him. They plan to get together, and she reassures him that Dangier, Malebouche, and Argus will not bother him. But successive troubles keep them apart; an epidemic, bad weather, fear of highway robbers, and then a gossip's report that the lady is making fun of him keep him from setting out for a reunion. By means of another dream, however, and a report from her confessor whom she sends as a messenger [and who ought to know], he is convinced of her faithfulness and sends her his apologies. She answers in a final letter, and the poet closes with an acrostic which seems to identify the lover as Guillaume and the lady as Peronelle d'Armentières.

Paulin Paris in his introduction to the *Voir Dit* explains Peronelle's consistent aggressiveness as resulting from customs of the time. In the thirteenth and fourteenth centuries, says Paris, young bachelors "abandonnaient assez volontiers au beau sexe le soin des premières avances.... On trouvera constamment dans le *Voir-Dit* la preuve de cette facon de procéder."[9] This is an amusing suggestion even if true. Actually, the backward and easily-daunted poet-lover portrayed in the *Voir Dit* is quite consistent with Machaut's unique narrator as he appears elsewhere,[10] so that the characterization of the lover in this poem probably does not reflect a general state of affairs in medieval France.

A connection of the *Voir Dit* with Chaucer's work has been seen in the analogue which its exemplum of Phebus and the crow offers to the Manciple's Tale, but no direct filiation has been shown.[11] Another analogue may be found in the narrator's taking up of a book toward the end of the poem in order to relieve his ennui:

Si que, pour moy desanuier,
Pris un livret à manier
Qu'on appelle Fulgencius,
Si trouvay Titus-Lyvius
Qui de Fortune descrisoit
L'image et ainsi disoit...   (ll. 8233-38)

He then describes the story in the book. Chaucer similarly at the beginning of the *Duchess* reads a book when he finds himself afflicted with sleeplessness:

So when I saw I might not slepe
Til now late, this other night,

Upon my bed I sat upright
And bad oon reche me a book,
A romaunce, and he it me tok
To rede, and drive the night away;
For me thoughte it beter play
Then play either at ches or tables.
And in this bok were written fables
That clerkes had in olde tyme,
And other poets, put in rime...   (ll. 44-54)

Mild desperation, then, inspires both lovers to read the books, and both read classical stories which they narrate in the poems. There is no diction which would show Chaucer's use of the French passage here, but among the *dits* antedating the *Duchess* it is easily the nearest analogue to Chaucer's reading of a book.

Sypherd stated that "the introductory device of reading a book" is one of "the regular features of a love-vision," but then cited only Froissart's *Espinette amoreuse* to support this statement.[12] In this *dit*, which will be discussed in a later chapter, the poet encounters a lady who is reading the romance of *Cléomadès*. The two talk and then read the romance to each other, but the story read is not narrated in the poem. Dissatisfied with Sypherd's rather superficial parallel, Marshall W. Stearns found in Guillaume de Lorris' statements about the *Somnium Scipionis* a more likely "ultimate source" of Chaucer's book. Stearns' searchings revealed no other analogues, and he concluded that there was no genuine convention established for this feature before Chaucer.[13] His conclusion seems basically sound, though he did fail to note the passage in *Voir Dit* which presents better evidence for a convention than he or Sypherd brought forward.

If it could be assumed that Chaucer read the *Voir Dit* this passage might very well be seen as a source for the *Duchess*. But beyond this congruency and the Phebus *exemplum*, very little in the *Voir Dit* suggests Chaucer. The case is somewhat better for Chaucer's having read and used the *Dit de l'Alerion*. Edith Rickert, in arguing for an allegorical interpretation of the *Parliament of Fowls*, notes the precedent of the *Alerion's* bird

85

allegory.[14] The parallel is sufficiently strong to make a connection between the poems probable. Chaucer in the *Parliament* distinguishes various kinds of falcons as courtly lovers, who contrast with the other birds who have no knowledge of the ways of gentle folk; likewise, Machaut's allegorized and genteel representatives of lady-loves in *Alerion* are all of the falcon family. Among Chaucer's courtly birds are the sparrowhawk, merlin, and formel and tercel eagles, which correspond to Machaut's sparrowhawk, gerfalcon, and two kinds of eagle.

An extrinsic reason for believing that Chaucer read the *Alerion* is that it appears in most Machaut manuscripts in the midst of poems from which Chaucer obviously borrowed; usually it appears just after the *Dit dou Lyon* and preceding the *Confort d'Ami* and *Fonteinne amoreuse*.[15] Among the first eight of Machaut's long works Chaucer used five in the *Duchess*. He later drew on the *Confort d'Ami* (ll. 2452-55) for some details in the *House of Fame* (ll. 534-540), and if it is conceded that *Alerion* influenced the *Parliament*, then only the slight and derivative *Dit dou Vergier* among the love narratives before *Voir Dit* (1364) left no mark on Chaucer's poems. In the light of this use of other works, it would be remarkable if Chaucer had read and then failed to use *Voir Dit*, as long and pretentious as that work is. The inference that he did not read it helps to construct hypothetically a manuscript collection of Machaut which Chaucer might have read in the 1360's before writing the *Duchess*. Such a manuscript presumably included the first eight long poems, the last of which—the *Fonteinne amoreuse*—was written in 1360, and also contained many of the lyrics. If it did not include *Voir Dit* the manuscript was probably assembled before that poem was written in 1363 or 1364. Though it may be that Chaucer met Machaut when he was a prisoner of war in France (early 1360), as Oliver F. Emerson suggests, this contact could not account for such a manuscript, considering the later composition of the *Fonteinne amoreuse*.[16] It is quite possible, on the other hand, that Froissart, whose *dits* depend heavily on his

86

older countryman, brought the supposed manuscript of Machaut's works to England when he began service at the English court in 1361.

In whatever way Chaucer became familiar with Machaut's works, he obviously was impressed, for in the *Book of the Duchess* he uses important features of narrative and detail and hundreds of individual lines from the poetry. After the *Duchess* Chaucer came under the influence of other writers and constantly experimented with new forms, so that the elegy contains the bulk of his borrowing from Machaut. But it cannot be said—as many have intimated—that Chaucer gradually purged his writings of the influence of contemporary love narrative. It more accurately may be stated that he absorbs and subsumes it. His specific uses of Machaut in subsequent poems are substantial —in the *House of Fame, Troilus and Criseyde,* and especially the *Legend of Good Women.* His reading of Machaut also seems to have widened, for he used the late *Dit de la Marguerite* (1364) in the *Legend of Good Women* and probably the *Prise d'Alexandrie* (1369 or 1370) in the Monk's Tale, the latter of which he could hardly have had access to before composing the *Duchess.*[17] What is more significant, Chaucer's works throughout his career continue to evidence the influence of Machaut. This, among other things, the analysis of Machaut's works in the next two chapters should suggest.

CHAPTER V

THE JUDGMENT POEMS OF MACHAUT

Though the discussions in previous chapters have treated the *dits amoreux* as if they belonged to a selfcontained tradition descending from the *Roman de la Rose*, literary influences from outside this tradition fundamentally affected many of these works. It has not seemed especially relevant before this to discuss such complicating influences; but one can hardly talk about Machaut's judgment poems without taking note of the group of love-debate narratives, antedating the *Roman de la Rose*, represented by such poems as the Latin *Council of Remiremont* and *Phyllis and Flora*.[1] Several of the poems previously discussed, notably the *Fablel, De Venus*, and the *Messe des oisiaus*, are strongly indebted to these works, both for their debates and for other features such as the elaborate love rituals and the depiction of the Castle of Love.

The literary debate goes back at least to Theocritus and Vergil. However, it is unnecessary to consider here the development of the form before *Phyllis and Flora*,[2] the best-known of the longer medieval debate narratives and probably the one with which Machaut was most familiar. The first part of this poem features a debate held between two young ladies one spring morning out in a meadow. It begins as an exchange of confidences, with Phyllis revealing that she is in love with a knight and Flora that she loves a clerk. The discussion grows into an argument on the merits of knights and clerks as lovers. The girls eventually decide to go to the court of Cupid to ask him to settle the question. The fine mounts which carry them to the castle of Cupid and the castle itself are described at length. After the god hears and weighs their arguments, he renders a judgment in favor of the clerk (such a decision being in accord with a clerk-poet's natural bias).

The basic plot of Machaut's first debate, the *Jugement dou Roy de Behaingne*, is quite similar to the plot of *Phyllis and Flora*. It begins with a lady and a knight exchanging personal love stories, the exchange developing into a debate on a love question which they take to the king. The palace is described as they ride toward it. There, after hearing the arguments, the king decides the question. Plot similarities thus make it clear that Machaut's poem has a legitimate ancestor in *Phyllis and Flora*. There are integral features, nevertheless, which ally *Behaingne* to the *dits amoreux*: the first-person narrator who participates in the story, the use by the knight and the lady of the conventional love stories, and the active role of personifications.

Behaingne is probably the second in date of composition of Machaut's longer works. In contrast to the evident lack of inspiration in the first (*Dit dou Vergier*), *Behaingne* is perhaps the most original and interesting of all his *dits*.[3] The distinctiveness of the poem is indicated even in the versification, which differs from the octosyllabic couplet form which Machaut and the other writers of the *dits amoreux* normally employ. Here Machaut uses a four-line unit in which the first three lines have ten syllables and the fourth four syllables, the units being tied together by the rhyme pattern, aaab-bbbc-cccd, etc.

The debate which occupies the first half of *Behaingne* is overheard by the narrator of the poem one morning when he walks out and follows a bird into a *destour* filled with trees and flowers. As he sits there listening to the birds singing, a lady approaches leading a dog and a small girl; from the other direction a knight comes toward her; the poet, unobserved, watches. When the lady fails to salute the knight, he reproaches her and she apologizes, explaining that she is sadder than anyone ever was. He replies that he would like to hear her troubles, since he does not think that any human could endure as much pain as he has. They thereupon agree to exchange stories to see whose trouble is worse.

She tells of the death of her lover (ll. 125-205). Bonne Amour, she explains, gave her a knight who was the flower of pleasant conduct: true, loyal, and secret. Their hearts made such a perfect pair that neither ever acted contrary to the other; but now, she asserts, she will never have comfort till Death takes her—Death, who did a great wrong when he did not seize her with her lover. The lady faints at this point, and the knight revives her with some dew he gathers from the grass. He gently admonishes her for weakness of heart, and tells her that her trouble is easier to relieve than his own.

His is a story of betrayal (ll. 261-860). From the time he had the use of reason, he explains, he devoted himself to Bonne Amour and prayed for a mistress whom he could serve. One day he came into the company of many beautiful ladies, where he saw one who outshone the rest as the sun outshines the moon. She danced so daintily, sang so prettily, and laughed and deported herself so graciously that he knew there was never such a treasure. To support the apparent extravagance of his praise, the knight recites her physical beauties from hair of golden thread down to arched, rounded, well-jointed, finely shod feet; he estimates her age at fourteen and a half. After he saw her, her image was imprinted permanently on his heart, but for a long time he was unable to confess his love for fear of refusal. Finally, Bel Acueil, Dous Regard, and Dous Espoirs encouraged him to the point that he spoke to her and begged for mercy. The beloved replied, however, that since Amour had caused his trouble, he should complain to Amour, not to her. But the sweetness of her look when she turned away said, "Ami, I love you very amorously," and this sustained him. Subsequently, after he had served her for a long time without reward, she became convinced that he

90

worked only for her honor and good, and granted him her love. The knight reigned in joy a long time, but then Fortune turned her wheel and he fell into the mud. Fortune could do this because God and Nature had given his beloved so much beauty they had forgotten to give her loyalty.

The knight's conclusion that the lady's troubles are joy and perfect sweetness beside his leads to an indecisive exchange between the two (ll. 861-1175). The lady retorts that he still has hope that by serving faithfully he may have relief again, but she has no possible remedy. He rejoins that he has no more hope than she, for his beloved has no loyalty, without which she will always change: Nature conquers education; the wolf always returns to the wood. One can possess only a poor part of the heart of his beloved. The lady can forget her *ami*, since it is customary to forget soon after the body is buried, but he sees his beloved often with her new lover, which almost drives him crazy. It gives him a hundred times more vexation for her than for himself, since many will know that she is false. Thus the knight believes his sorrow to be greater than the lady's, and he expresses a wish that they knew someone to judge the question truly. She agrees readily.

Both having stated their cases, the scene is set for the judgment section which occupies the remainder of the poem (ll. 1176-2079). The narrator, discovered by the lady's dog, comes out of hiding to recommend for judge Jean of Luxembourg, the King of Bohemia —a prince who surpasses Alexander in largess and Hector in prowess, and who knows the problems of love better than Ovid. Theruepon all three travel to the beautiful Castle of Derbui, where they find the king listening to the reading of a tale of Troy. Courtiers such as Honneur and Courtoisie, who personify the virtues of the king, surround him. The court listens to the stories of the lovers, and Loiauté, Amour, Juenesse, and Raison all agree that the knight is the greater sufferer, though they debate about the wisdom of his continued loyalty to the lady (Raison thinks that he should have forgotten about her when she proved false). In accord with his counsellor's opinion the king decrees in the knight's favor, then hospitably refuses to grant the two debaters leave to go. Rather he entertains them eight days before having them escorted home with presents of horses, harness, jewels, and silver.

The impressive line-for-line contributions of *Behaingne* to the *Book of the Duchess* have been well documented in Professor Kittredge's articles.[4] In using this poem for the Black Knights' complaints and story, Chaucer adapted the diction of more than 250 lines. Only *Remede de Fortune*, of which Chaucer uses 200 lines for the *Duchess*, exercises a comparable influence on the diction. But the mark of *Remede de Fortune* on the narrative is in no way comparable to that of *Behaingne*, for the whole section of Chaucer's poem in which the Black Knight participates combines elements of the situations and stories of the two despondent lovers in *Behaingne*.[5] For example, both the Black Knight and the lady of *Behaingne* appear on the scene so lost in sorrow that they are unconscious of the approach of others. Both are physically stunned by their individual sorrows, and both tell about the deaths of loved ones. The Black Knight is like the knight of *Behaingne* in believing that his story is worse than his auditor can understand, and the stories themselves have much in common. Each knight tells how he served Love from youth and first saw his lady in a crowd of beautiful women. Each describes the lady in proper rhetorical form, from head to foot. And each relates how he finally summoned courage to approach his lady, only to be rebuffed. Eventually, by dint of long service, each was granted grace and lived in joy until Fortune turned her wheel.

In addition to these parallels in story to *Behaingne*, which Chaucer's heavy verbal borrowings show not to be fortuitous, there is also a significant debate element in the *Duchess*—found in the exchanges between the dreamer and the Black Knight—which allies it to Machaut's judgement poems, particularly to *Behaingne*. The dreamer tells the knight that his beloved cannot be as wonderful and valuable as he thinks she is, and is certainly not worth suicide:

"But ther is no man alyve her
Wolde for a fers make this woo!"   (ll. 740-741)

The Knight counters repeatedly:

"Thow wost ful lytel what thow menest;
I have lost more than thou wenest."[6]

But the dreamer simply will not succumb to the knight's insistence that no one could have as fine as lady as he had. He would argue that there are many fine ladies around. This discussion is in effect a debate about the importance of the lady to the lover, involving a proper *demande d'amour*: Are there circumstances, such as death and desertion, which make it proper to abandon one's love? The question is like the one debated at the end of *Behaingne* where Raison and Loiauté assert, contrary to Amour and Jeunesse, that the knight of the poem should have ceased to love when his lady took a new lover. One must adjust his loyalty to the situation, they claim—a point of view which the pragmatic dreamer of the *Duchess* would no doubt have supported.

The debate element is essential to *Behaingne* in providing the occasion for lengthy dialogue; so also in Chaucer's work it provides impetus to the discussion between the Black Knight and the dreamer, and to the narration of the Black Knight's story. The result in both poems is that discussion, rather than simple description and monologue, is fostered. On the other hand too much emphasis could be placed on the debate element in the *Duchess*, since the narrator is basically more a comforter than a dialectician. As a comforter he has different antecedents in Machaut, as the next chapter will show.

The second of Machaut's debate poems, the *Jugement dou Roy de Navarre*, is only a minor source for the diction of the *Duchess*,[7] but among Machaut's poems it presents the best-developed picture of his narrator, who has some interesting similarities to Chaucer's poetic *persona*. Furthermore, it is an important antecedent of the *Legend of Good Women*, and the sequence it forms with *Behaingne* presents a significant parallel to the sequence of Chaucer's early works.

Since *Navarre* is a sequel and palinode to *Behaingne*, it is invariably placed in the manuscripts right after the earlier debate, though the composition of *Remede de Fortune, Dit dou Lyon*, and *Dit de l'Alerion* probably intervened between the debates. *Navarre* clearly was written in the post-Plague year of 1349. Its 4212 lines make it over twice as long as *Behaingne*, with the many *exempla* which are related in *Navarre* accounting for its greater length. A point that distinguishes *Navarre* from the other Machaut *dits* is the fact that the narrator is openly identified by the poet's name; his speeches have the heading *Guillaume*, and the other characters address him by that name. Generally, in Machaut's poetry the narrator is anonymous, except for the identifications supplied by anagrams. Similarly in Chaucer's works the narrator is not identified as *Geffrey* except in the *House of Fame*.

The idealized setting of *Navarre's* main section contrasts vividly with the realism of the introduction (ll. 1-458), which has been described in Chapter I. Guillaume, locked in his room for months for fear of the Plague, considers the decay of the times. Suddenly his meditations are interrupted by music outside his window (ll. 461-464). He opens the casement and is told that the epidemic is over. It is spring. Feeling free to roam at large once again, he goes rabbit hunting, a very noble pursuit, he asserts. While he is intent on the hunt a squire rides up and summons him to the presence of a noble lady, later identified as Bonneurté. The poet envisions an affair of gallantry, but the lady greets him with an accusation of treachery to women, since he had said in the *Jugement dou Roy Behaingne* that the knight suffers more than the lady. Guillaume stubbornly reaffirms the position he took in *Behaingne* and suggests that the question be put to a judge once more; the lady agrees and chooses the King of Navarre to hear the case. Entering the king's castle, the lady is received almost as mistress of the manor, and is accompanied by twelve female attendants, personifications such as Congnoissance, Raison, Attemprance, and Franchise. The king, having agreed to hear the case with the help of some of the lady's retinue, leads her up to sit with him.

The case is argued at great length (ll. 1629-3412). The lady and her attendants narrate a series of *exempla* to prove that the death of the loved one is the greatest tragedy of love, and that the lady rather than the man is the greater sufferer in love. Guillaume rebuts with some *exempla* of his own, and in his peroration goes so far as to assert that there is no constancy in women:

> Qu'en cuer de femme n'a riens ferme
> Rien seur, rien d'estableté. (ll. 3020-21)

The attendants then attack Guillaume more vigorously, which leads him to foolhardy facetiousness: he suggests that they all might speak together to speed the pleading of the case. Eventually the lady calls for a judgment, and in the long conclusion (ll. 3413-4212) the king and his counsellors pronounce judgement and fix the sentence. They decide that Guillaume's *exempla* are not convincing and that he is guilty of three misdeeds: the composition of the heretical *Behaingne*; persistence in error, as shown in his arguing with the ladies; and the derogation of the character of women by impugning their constancy. Guillaume kneels before the king, who takes the poet's hands and releases them three times in token of his threefold guilt and the triple penance he is assigned. He must write a *lay*, a *chanson*, and a *balade*.

In most Machaut manuscripts the *Lay de Plour*, a lament by a lady over the death of her loved one, follows *Navarre*. It seems obviously designed to satisfy the first penance. The prescribed *chanson* and *balade*, if they were written, remain unidentified. The supplementary *lay*, in its partial satisfaction of the penance assigned, has an obvious relationship to Chaucer's incomplete series of legends of women martyred for love, also written to atone for injustice to women in previous poetry. Several other elements reinforce the parallel between Machaut's second judgement poem and the *Legend of Good Women*.[8] In both narratives the poet is represented as having offended women in his works; as Machaut is indicted by Bonneurté for having written *Behaingne*, so is Chaucer accused by the God of Love for his translation of the *Romance of the Rose* and particularly for *Troilus*:

> And of Creseyde thou hast seyd as the lyste,
> That maketh men to wommen lasse triste,
> That ben as trewe as ever was any steel. (F. 332-334)

Furthermore, in subject and purpose the series of *exempla* cited by the ladies in proof of the virtue and suffering of women for Love is similar to Chaucer's collection of legends.[9]

An analogy also exists between the sequences formed by Machaut's two debate poems and by three of Chaucer's works. *Behaingne* is concerned with the tragedies of two lovers; one has suffered a bereavement and the other has been betrayed by a woman who is perfect except that she lacks constancy. Chaucer's *Duchess*, which deals with a bereaved lover, and *Troilus and Criseyde*, which concerns a jilted knight, offer parallels to these tragedies. And just as Machaut's *Navarre* is designed to make amends for the injustices to women performed in *Behaingne*, so Chaucer's *Legend* aims at atonement for *Troilus*. Thus there exists an intriguing coincidence of subject and sequence between the works of the poets. The comparisons between the narratives of *Behaingne* and the *Duchess* and between *Navarre* and the *Legend* are particularly striking, and are supported by evident borrowing. At the same time the parallel between the story of Troilus and the story of Machaut's betrayed knight is not wholly superficial or wholly assignable to matters of convention. In each case there is the perfectly courteous knight, the eminently desirable lady, a difficult courtship, a period of happiness, and finally a betrayal when the lady turns out to lack only the virtue of constancy. Both jilted lovers even hear the voice of reason afterwards (Raison in *Behaingne* and Pandarus in *Troilus*) telling them to forget about the lady since she has acted traitorously. Of course the source for *Troilus* is Boccaccio, but the analogues between *Behaingne* and *Troilus* and between the sequence formed by Machaut's judgement poems and the three works of Chaucer at least provide food for speculation about the germinal stage in Chaucer's creations. It is certainly possible that Machaut's model helped to suggest subject and sequence to the English poet.

For the Chaucerian probably the most significant aspect of *Navarre* is the well-developed picture it presents of the individualized narrator of Machaut's later *dits*, a figure that provides a significant precedent for Chaucer's narrator, who first appears in the *Book of the Duchess*.

Though some development may be found, Chaucer's narrator is reasonably consistent throughout his work. In the *Duchess* he is an unidealized lover whose lack of success in love has made him "a mased thyng," suffering from "suche fantasies" that he does not know what to do. To help himself sleep he reads, since he loves reading better than games; and his reading leads him in jest to make a comic prayer to Morpheus, in which he promises Morpheus such appropriate thank-offerings as a feather-bed of pure white dove's down and a sound-proofed bed-chamber. When the gamesome prayer is successful, in his dream he whimsically chases a little dog down a path, then clownishly stands hat in hand before the Black Knight and gently offers his help. After the elegy proper gets under way, the whimsical nature of the narrator is appropriately submerged because of the subject matter. But the poet has already presented a figure with a potential for such ludicrous postures in later poems as being dangled by an eagle several thousand feet above the earth or being shoved by Scipio through the gates of Paradise. He is an awkward, bookish clerk, inept in love, with a puckish sense of humor which often exercises itself at his own expense.

97

As with his General Prologue, so with his humorous narrator, no single work or author can be said to provide Chaucer's original. There are many possible partial sources. Perhaps Chaucer's narrator owes something to the poets of the Old French *pastourelles* who as often as not depicted their first-person representatives as being verbally abused by the *bergères* whom they accost, or physically threatened and maltreated by the boyfriends, Robin or Perrin. No doubt the humor associated with Chrétien de Troyes' depictions—notably his heroes—has something in common with the comicality of Chaucer's *persona*. But the *dits amoreux* offer French precedents of more certain influence.

In Guillaume de Lorris' *Roman de la Rose*, the great progenitor, the narrator assuredly has humorous aspects: he tells with amusing straightforwardness how Dangier bullied him and how Raison wasted her good advice on him. In ensuing *dits*, also, the narrators often have comparably droll reactions. But almost everything about these narrators pertains to the generic lover; they are not individualized. It remained for Machaut to endow the narrator in the *dits amoreux* with a distinctive and clearly comic personality, ostensibly the poet's own. Despite John L. Lowes' statement that he found only "two mild essays at humor" in all his reading of Machaut's work,[10] Machaut manifested a fully developed sense of comedy repeatedly in his *dits*, and Professor Lowes would have had only to consider the narrator of his later poems to find many examples of humor.

In *Behaingne*, which is very early, the narrator has a small, though partially comic, role. It is humorous when the lady's little dog discovers the narrator and sinks its teeth into his clothes, and when this delights him because it gives him an excuse for suggesting that the King of Bohemia judge the debate. *Remede de Fortune* is still early, but there are two episodes toward the end of this poem which mark a tendency to individualize and make comic the narrator. When Amant, the narrator, hesitates on his return to his lady's home, Esperance appears to him a second time, and, in place of the high-style comfort she had offered before, she excoriates him, accusing him of being afraid of his own shadow and of having the acuity and understanding of a caged bird (ll. 3065-3180). And there is irony in the contrast of the lady with Amant after she has verbally acceded to his plea; her ambiguous actions and ingenious explanations suggest that the puzzled and naive narrator has been granted a practical and pragmatic lady who is more than a match for him. The narrator in the *Dit dou Lyon* also is somewhat funny in his terrified reaction to the lion's sudden charge, but the drollery connected with lion's activities overshadows the persona of the poet in that work.

It is only in *Navarre*, when the poet and the narrator are explicitly equated, that Machaut's conception of his poetic self is developed. He presents himself as frankly cowardly, but at the same time headstrong, conceited, and suffering from the delusion that he is a man of noble behavior and strong attraction for women. At the beginning of the narrative, after he discusses the Plague and other current calamities, Guillaume is seen to be most timid about venturing out for fear of the Plague; people are dancing in the streets before he even opens his shutters. When the outdoors are safe, he decides to do something to promote his honor; for him, it turns out, honor resides in hunting rabbits:

> En celle cusançon estoie
> Pour honneur a quoy je tendoie.
> Cusançon avoie et desir
> Que je peüsse, a mon loisir,
> Aucuns lievres a point sousprendre,
> Par quoy je les peüsse prendre.   (ll. 501-506)

Exactly what kind of rabbit Guillaume had in mind to hunt—a little animal or an amorous woman[11]—is questionable and probably purposely ambiguous. In any event he is immediately ready for action when a squire rides up to summon him to his mistress; he is sure that he is being pursued by a fair damsel for amorous purposes. The squire, in a practical-joking spirit,

99

compounds Guillaume's confusion by telling him that the lady is a three-day ride from the hunting ground. Undaunted by this news, the poet is ready to start at once and ride day and night. But he follows the squire for only a short distance before they come into the presence of Bonneurté, with whom Guillaume finds an argument rather than a love affair.

In debating before the king, as already shown, the poet argues tenaciously and outrageously. He supports his case with one particularly tasteless story about a young man who promises his mistress never to remove her ring from his finger. When she is required by her husband to produce the ring, in desperation she sends to the lover for it; he thereupon cuts off his finger and sends it with the ring so as not to break his promise. Finding such an *exemplum* disgusting, Bonneurté's counsellors strenuously upbraid Guillaume for his lapses in taste; but he is quite blind to his weakness and persists in using poor judgment. When the ladies attack him in unison, he sarcastically requests that they present their arguments all at once to save time; and in the face of the obviously good relations of the judge with the ladies, he condemns women for their faithlessness and fickleness, praising the character of men at their expense. He loses the argument, of course, is well chided by Raison for his obtuseness, and is forced to submit humbly to his punishment.

The narrator of the *Fonteinne amoreuse* is potentially the same kind of person as Guillaume is in *Navarre*. His anti-heroic nature shows up in the opening passages when he describes himself as jumping under the covers of his bed for fear of a ghost. The cause of his fear proves to be a lover who is complaining next door. The narrator proceeds to justify his timidity by stating almost proudly that it is as proper for clerks to be cowardly as it is for knights to be brave; he even discusses the superior safety (for the cowardly) of keeping with the leader during a battle. In the remainder of the *Fonteinne amoreuse*, however, the young noble-man who is the complaining lover occupies the center of the stage, so that the character of the narrator is subordinated and there are only hints of his individuality after the opening section.

Machaut's and Chaucer's narrators are certainly not the same characters—the very development which Machaut initiated was the endowment of the narrator with a distinctive personality. But the conceptions of the two poets have much in common: both narrators are unheroic, clerkly, comic types, who often provide humor at their own expense. Both contrast with the courtly figures of their poems; in *Navarre* Guillaume contrasts with the king as does the dreamer in the *Duchess* with the Black Knight. Thus, one origin of Chaucer's poetic persona is found in Machaut's work, particularly in *Navarre*.

It is perhaps surprising that Froissart did not create an individualized narrator, especially in two poems which clearly imitate Machaut's, the *Paradys d'Amours* and the *Espinette amoreuse*. The characterizations of the narrators in these works are, however, quite consistent with the conventional picture of the courtly lover. There is humor in the *Paradys d'Amours* in the way Amant is confronted by Esperance and Plaisance after he complained about their treatment of him; and the conversation he has with his lady at the end of the poem has a degree of witty sparkle. In the *Espinette* too some of the narrator's actions and reactions are funny because of their extremity. But in neither poem is found the drollery of Chaucer's narrator or the anti-heroism of Machaut's.[12]

In the final analysis, though, Froissart was exercising sound poetic judgement in *Paradys* and *Espinette*. The narrators in these poems are the central figures involved in conventional love stories, and an individualized lover has no place in the center of such a story. In Machaut's *Navarre* and *Fonteinne amoreuse*, as in Chaucer's *Duchess*, the narrator is not a major figure in the love situations, so that individualization of him does not detract from the idealized stories. The primary love figures in these works, it will be noticed, are quite conventional. Similarly, the unconventional story and unorthodox attitude toward love of the narrator of the *Dit de l'Alerion* vitiates the idealized aura which should surround a *dit amoreux*; so also the narrator of the *Voir Dit*, a figure consistent with the individualized narrator of earlier poems of Machaut, appears ludicrous when required to play the romantic lead. A certain amount of interest attaches to the narrator himself in *Voir Dit*, but the conventional trappings of the *dits amoreux*, the specialized diction, the classical *exempla*, the lyric set-pieces all become pointless and oppressive when made to revolve around such a lover.

Individualized, unidealized lovers in conventional narrative settings make parodies of the stories. If the standard trappings are used for ostensibly humorous purposes, as in the Merchant's Tale or the Miller's Tale, then such parodies can supply sufficient humor to bear the story's weight. But in the full-dress treatment of a *dit amoreux* or of a *Troilus and Criseyde*, neither a comic narrator nor a Pandarus can successfully fill the lover's role. Pandarus is more interesting than Troilus, but Troilus, despite his woodenness, must play his own part. An individualized Guillaume can perform successfully as the central figure of *Navarre* because there is no important love story in the poem, but rather the presentation of a question of love. In *Behaingne*, on the other hand, it is because he is a witness rather than a participant that the characterization of the narrator need not subserve the conventions. Likewise in the *Duchess* Chaucer has freedom to develop his dreamer as an individual because he is a spectator and listener, uninvolved in the love tragedy.

The debate poems taken up in this chapter thus provide impressive precedents to the *Book of the Duchess*: *Behaingne* for the Black Knight's situation and story, *Navarre* for the character of the narrator, and both poems for the debate element in the work. It is not, however, to Machaut's *judgments* that the *Duchess* has the greatest affinity, but rather to his poems of complaint and comfort—notably the *Fonteinne amoreuse*. These provide the subject of the next chapter.

CHAPTER VI

MACHAUT'S POEMS OF COMPLAINT AND COMFORT

The bulk of Chaucer's borrowing for the *Book of the Duchess* was made from five French *dits amoreux*. Two of these have already been taken up, the *Roman de la Rose* and the *Jugement dou Roy de Behaingne*. Of the other three, two will be dealt with in this chapter, Machaut's *Remede de Fortune* and *Dit de la Fonteinne amoreuse*; and the third, Froissart's *Paradys d'Amours*, will be considered in Chapter VII. All three of these works have the same basic narrative pattern of lover's complaint answered by a comforter, but they make their contributions to quite distinct sections of Chaucer's poem: the *Paradys d'Amours* is the main source for the dream machinery, the *Fonteinne amoreuse* for the story of Seys and Alcyone, and *Remede de Fortune*, along with *Behaingne*, accounts for a large part of the Black Knight's complaints and story. The *Roman de la Rose*, as has been noted, is the primary source for the description of the garden. An outline shows graphically how these works fit into the rather neat pattern of Chaucer's borrowing:

I. The frame-story outside the dream.
   A. The dream machinery (*Duchess*, ll. 1-61; 221-290; 1325-34):
      Froissart's *Paradys d'Amours* is major source.
   B. The Seys and Alcyone story (ll. 62-220):
      Machaut's *Dit de la Fonteinne amoreuse*.

II. The frame within the vision, containing the description of the garden and the hunt (ll. 291-442; 1311-24): *Roman de la Rose*.

103

Despite the great importance of *Behaingne* and the *Rose* to Chaucer's poem, the *Duchess* can be classed most appropriately with its other three sources as a poem of "complaint and comfort." The concluding three chapters of this study take up the development of this type of narrative from Machaut into the fifteenth century. Such a consideration makes clear the interrelationships of these works and helps to establish their sequence, particularly with regard to the *Book of the Duchess*.

The complaint-and-comfort *dits* provide a narrative setting for the lover's *complaints* which became quite popular with fourteenth-century poets. They had come to think of such complaints as comprising virtually a separate lyric genre, even though no particular form was assigned to them. Thus manuscripts of Machaut's works have a separate section entitled "Complaints," consisting of poems whose versification, while differing from that of other lyric types, is not standardized. Machaut did make a move toward fixing the versification by putting several of the complaints in sixteen-line stanzas of identical rhyme schemes, a structure which Froissart subsequently used in two of his complaints as did Chaucer in two stanzas of Anelida's complaint.[1] But the form was not generally adopted. Chaucer himself uses various kinds of stanzas in his works which are called complaints. In the *Duchess* the description of the Black Knight's lament is indicative of the poet's uncertainty as regards the complaint genre. The dreamer states initially that the knight

> made of ryme ten vers or twelve
> Of a *compleynte* to hymselve.   (ll. 463-464)

104

Then a few lines later he describes it as "lay, a maner song" (l. 471). The versification, however, hardly that of a *lay* or a *chanson*, seems quite individual.

In any event, the fact that the rhyme scheme of this eleven-line lyric differs from the rest of the *Duchess* shows that Chaucer did think of the complaint as a distinctive entity. Anelida's complaint likewise interrupts the rhyme-royal form of *Anelida and Arcite*. In the earlier development of the *dit amoreux*, however, the lover's complaint forms an undifferentiated part of a narrative. It is integrated into the couplets, even though it generally has the same content as later when the lament is set off by a separate form. Guillaume de Lorris' lover, on the occasion of his second repulse, presents a good short example of the earlier complaint incorporated into a narrative:

> Mar touchai la rose a mon vis
> E a mes iauz e a ma bouche,
> S'Amors ne suefre que j'i touche
> Tot de rechief autre feiee;
> Se j'ai la savor essaiee,
> Tant est graindre la covoitise
> Qui esprent mon cuer e atise.
> Or revendront plor e sospir,
> Longues pensees senz dormir,
> Friçons e pointes e complaintes.
> De teus dolors avrai je maintes,
> Car je sui en enfer cheoiz.
> Male Bouche soit maleoiz!
> Sa langue desleial e fausse
> M'a porchaciee ceste sausse.   (ll. 3782-96)

The lover in the *dit amoreux* can complain at any length about the unfairness of Love to him, the burning of Desire, the lack of Hope, the crimes of Dangier and Malebouche, and how these combine to make him tremble, weep, and become ill. Here he is unwontedly brief. A somewhat longer example is found elsewhere in Guillaume's section of the Rose, when the God of Love puts a hypothetical complaint in the lover's mouth (ll. 2449-2504) in the course of explaining to Amant the physical and mental anguish a lover goes through. These complaints, however, do not have the functional importance in the story which the complaint of Amant has near the beginning of Jean de Meun's continuation (ll. 4059-4220), for there the lament calls forth Raison to answer at considerable length. This complaint is thus a motivating force in the narrative, quite similar to Boethius' complaint at the beginning of the *Consolation* which evokes the comfort and instruction of Lady Philosophy.

In the *Romanz de la Poire*, as in Jean de Meun's part of the *Rose*, Raison appears to the lover in answer to his complaints about the hopelessness of his situation (ll. 1878-2015).[2] She soon disappears, however, when the lover disdains her advice. The complaint performs an even more essential narrative function in the *Fablel dou Dieu d'Amours* and *De Venus la Deese d'Amor*. The God of Love appears in the *Fablel* when the lover laments the seizure of his beloved by the dragon (strophes 56-58), and eventually the god pacifies the lover by rescuing the lady. A much longer complaint in *De Venus* (strophes 31-114) results in the appearance of the Goddess of Love, who takes the lover off to her castle where he is eventually awarded the lady.

The simple plot of complaint and remedy is used to bind together the narratives of the *Fablel* and *De Venus*, which are encumbered with descriptions of the Palace of Love and its activities. Essentially the same plot is used in Machaut's *Remede de Fortune*. When Amant in that poem, having suffered a reversal in his love affair, complains, Esperance appears to advise and comfort him, this help being ultimately efficacious. The complaint-and-comfort plot of *Remede de Fortune*, however, is no mere framework on which to hang episodes of tangential relevance as it tends to be in *De Venus* and the *Fablel*. It rather dominates and unifies Machaut's work, as it was to dominate and unify the series of poems which *Remede de Fortune* fathered. The first offspring was Machaut's own *Fonteinne amoreuse*. The two Machaut poems then combined to provide the basic influences on three poems of Froissart. The central situation of Chaucer's *Book of the Duchess*, furthermore, stems from *Fonteinne amoreuse*, and the same situation is used in *Songe vert* and two of Granson's poems. The discussion in the next three chapters attempts to make clear the important and interesting interrelationships of these works. The treatment of the two Machaut poems in this chapter shows moreover the final stages in the development of the *dit amoreux* to the point at which it was taken over by Chaucer.

In his long introduction to *Remede de Fortune*, Ernest Hoepffner emphasizes the didacticism of the poem; at bottom, he says, the poem "est un traité didactique sur Amour et Fortune, encadré dans le récit d'une aventure d'amour personelle au poète."[3] Hoepffner finds an Art of Love particularly at the beginning and end of the work. He argues that a further didactic purpose is manifested in the intercalation of eight lyric pieces—each of a different form—into the narrative of *Remede de Fortune*: "Il nous donne ici un tableau complet des principales formes lyriques qui étaient en usage dans la première moitié du xive siècle."[4] In the chronology of Machaut's *dits*, the poem evidently follows immediately after *Behaingne*, being written sometime before 1342. Its 4298 lines make it one of his longer works. Many of the speeches of the first-person narrator have the heading *Amant*, and he is thus referred to in the following summary.

Having enumerated to begin with twelve things which one must do to learn any art, Amant tells how his own works were inconstant till Amour gave his heart to a beautiful lady. He is now hers completely, he avers, though he could not love her enough had he the valor of Alexander or Hector, or the honor of Godfrey of Bouillon, or the beauty of Absalon, or the patience of Job, or the constancy of Judith and Socrates. From the beginning his character was improved by her and he served her, but he did not dare to let her know his love. To pass the time he took to writing poems about her; he recites a *lay* (ll. 431-680) in which he asks that Amour tell his lady how much he loves her. One day it chances that the lady sees this very lay and asks him who wrote it. Completely confused, he leaves her presence without answering and goes to the beautiful Parc de Hesdin, where he sits within a hedged enclosure beside a fountain. Blaming Amour and Fortune for his troubles, he decides to make a *complainte*, a *dit* of diverse rhymes and sad subject, against them.

In the lengthy complaint (ll. 905-1480) Amant attacks Fortune's inconstancy for three hundred lines; more than a hundred of these develop the comparison of Fortune with Nabogodonosor's idol with feet of clay. In the last part he berates Amour for beating him whom she holds prisoner, and accuses Amour of changing the dice on him. Pity sleeps, he claims, and Desire is awake, who like a hunting dog tracks him down to kill him. He closes the complaint with the wish that his soul be rendered up to his lady when he dies, and then he falls into a trance. Partially reviving after a while, he opens one eye and sees close to him a lady who is obviously more than human. The details of the appearance of this lady (who turns out to be Esperence), her efforts to help Amant, and what she has to say owe a great deal to Boethius' *Consolation*.[5] Her face shines with a brightness that pierces the cloud hanging over her head, and she exudes a sweet fragrance. He turns toward her but cannot speak, so she approaches and feels his pulse.

Esperence chides, corrects, and comforts Amant for the next thirteen hundred lines (1585-2892). First she points out to him that he has no right to hope for anything from his lady other than that which Souvenir and Douce Pensée can give him, since his beloved's least reward is worth many times his merit. Then she scolds him for being in his attack on Amour like a dog who barks at the one who has helped him. In his lay, she points out, he asked Amour to reveal his love to the lady, and Amour did this by making him unable to speak when she questioned him about the lay. His behavior had been such as a false Amant could not feign; Amour, therefore, had caused him to wear the blue shield of true love.[6] He displayed this shield till his spirit failed him, Esperence continues, and now she will restore it to him. To begin his recovery she sings him a forty-eight line *chanson royal*, and then she places on his finger a ring whose coolness awakens him completely from his trance. Esperence, still there, identifies herself by name and states that she is the comfort, castle, and fortress of lovers, their physician and their refuge. Amant in turn celebrates her sweetness, which no one could calculate even if he were a hundred thousand times more subtle than Arismetique, Pytagoras, Musique, Michalus, Milesius, and Orpheus. Before parting Esperence tells the lover at length in Boethian terms how to defend himself. She concludes that instead of depending on Fortune he should put himself in the way of Bonneurté, the perfect good which comes from the Lord above, who is the beginning and the end, three in one. Amant should not think, however, that she forbids him to love, for true lovers rely on virtue. Let him go now to his beloved without fear. After having sung a *balade* about Amour, she disappears.

Amant leaves the garden, noticing now the birds singing in thirty thousand places, their mouths agape, so that the whole wood resounds. As he walks happily along, he sings a *balade*,[7] but suddenly he stops, bewildered as to what to do. Esperence appears and scolds him roundly for not trusting in her help. Amant thereupon kneels in the middle of the path and makes a twelve-stanza prayer to Amour and Esperence (ll. 3205-3348); then he proceeds confidently to his lady's home, where a *carole* is in progress.

The rest of the poem (ll. 3376-4298) is occupied with the fulfillment of the promise of Esperence. At the *carole* Amant sings a *virelay* which is appropriately addressed to a lady from whom the lover can no longer hide his love. When he is led aside by the lady after the *carole*, Amant confesses his devotion and tells how Esperence has emboldened him to speak, for he would not dare to ask her for love or any other thing on his own. She

109

responds that he is right, for he who climbs higher than he should, falls from a higher place than he would wish. But she will not refuse the wish of Esperence, she adds, so she accepts his love and grants her own to him. They go to Mass and afterwards have dinner, at which the servants babble in French, Breton, German, Lombard, English, Provençal, Norman, and many other languages. After dinner minstrels perform; Machaut names thirty-two instruments on which they play. By the time wine and spices are served it is almost *nones* (3 p. m.), the time for leave-taking. Before parting Amant and his lady exchange rings and he walks away singing a *rondelet* about how he has left his heart behind. But when he returns later on she hardly looks at him, for which he reproaches her bitterly. She responds lightly that she must *bien celer* their relationship, and he perforce accepts the explanation. Machaut concludes the poem at this point, giving his name in an anagram and expressing the hope that his lady will read this *dit* with good heart and happy countenance.

Though many lines of the *Book of the Duchess* translate the language of *Remede de Fortune*, Chaucer generally converts to very different uses the phrases and lines he takes over from this work. Some of the passages descriptive of Esperence, for example, are used by Chaucer for the description of the deceased Duchess. As a result, the influence of this work of Machaut accounts for only one substantial narrative element of Chaucer's poem, the Black Knight's complaint against Fortune.[8] *Remede de Fortune's* primary influence on the *Duchess* is exercised through an intermediary, Machaut's other poem of complaint and comfort, the *Dit de la Fonteinne amoreuse*, which I shall take up shortly.

Before considering the *Fonteinne*, the work which forms the main connecting link of the *dits* with the *Duchess*, it may be salutary to review the development which has taken place from the *Roman de la Rose* to *Remede de Fortune*. For the allegorized setting of the Garden of Love in the *Rose*, a literal house and an actual garden have been substituted. In place of the one-sided

110

Amant and Amie, whose actions relate only to the "old dance" of Love, the lovers of *Remede de Fortune* participate in such other human activities as eating, playing games, and attending Mass. Allegorical narrative also has almost disappeared from *Remede de Fortune*. Esperence does act to give hope to the lover, but she also says many things in defending Amour and Fortune which are hardly appropriate to a personification of Hope. The reader comes to look upon Esperence, then, as a kindly supernatural female being rather than an embodiment of an abstract power contained in Amant's psyche.

The attitude toward love is also much more ambiguous in *Remede de Fortune* than it was in Guillaume de Lorris' poem. In the *Rose* the lover dreams of being naked in bed with his lady. In *Remede de Fortune* Esperence tells Amant that he should concern himself with the perfect good which comes from God, and that a true lover should rely on virtue, rather than Fortune, to win the lady. Machaut gives no indication in this poem that the *merci* which the lover expects is other than innocent, though the reader is free to suspect what he wishes, and the tradition might lead him to suspect quite a bit. In one of his lays, however, Machaut confirms that according to his conception *merci* may consist of as little response on the lady's part as Dante was contented with.[9]

Along with the movement away from personification and allegory, and the increasing ambiguity in attitude toward love manifested in *Remede de Fortune*, this poem also reflects the increasing use of rhetoric and ornament discussed in an earlier chapter as a tendency of the *dits amoreux*. The wordy complaint of the narrator and the lengthy answer of Esperence involve long sections of lament, opprobrium, encouragement, and praise. The long lecture of Amour in the *Roman de la Rose*, by contrast, is devoted in large part to specific instructions concerning behavior and etiquette, and to narrative prediction to the lover's future life. The numerous lyric set-pieces of *Remede de Fortune*, furthermore, have no counterparts in Guillaume de Lorris' work.

111

Such developments, in some respects carried further, are reflected in Machaut's *Dit de la Fonteinne amoreuse*, which is closely related to *Remede de Fortune*. The characters of the lover and the poet are even more realistic and well-rounded; no personifications participate in the story; and there is no apparent trace of allegory. Almost no question exists, furthermore, of the moral respectability of the love portrayed, for an anagram tells us that Machaut made the poem for Jean, Duc de Berry, and the lady must be his new young wife, Jeanne d'Armagnac, since the poem was written within a year after Jean's marriage to her. The fact that the narrator in *Fonteinne amoreuse* is an observer, rather than the Amant of the poem, frees his character from the stereotype of the tradition and facilitates its individualization.

The subject matter of the *Fonteinne amoreuse* indicates that it was written on the occasion of the departure of the twenty-year-old Duc de Berry for England in 1360, where he was to serve as a hostage under the terms of the Treaty of Brétigny. The narrative deals with the lover's unhappiness at the prospect of enforced separation from his beloved and the consolation he is accorded in a dream. Reflecting this pattern of distress and consolation are the main lyric pieces of the poem: a *complaint* of 800 lines near the beginning with the same stanza form as in *Remede de Fortune*; and a set-piece of 320 lines toward the end, entitled "Le Confort de l'amant et de la dame," also in the sixteen-line complaint stanza. Of these balancing lyrics Hoepffner says that, "L'une, en effet, expose les tristesses, les craintes, les douleurs de l'amant malheureux, l'autre réfute un à un tous les arguments présentés précédemment et réunit tous les raisonnements susceptibles de redresser le courage abattu de l'amant."[10]

In the first fifty-four lines of the work, the poet states that he writes to honor his lady, and he identifies himself anagrammatically along with the one for whom he "made this book" (*Guillaumes de Machaut* and *Jean duc Berry e Overngne*). Then he relates how one night, overhearing someone complaining and sighing very loudly, he imagines there is a ghost outside and he trembles

112

and sweats for fear. Finally realizing, however, that the voice is coming from another building, he goes to the window and hears the words, "Goodbye, my lady, I am going away, leaving only my heart with you. But before I go I will make you a complaint." The eavesdropping poet thereupon lights a candle and prepares his writing equipment to transcribe the complaint.

The lover begins the fifty-stanza complaint (ll. 235-1034) by stating that he lives by his lady's looks, and now that he must go away he does not know how he will survive. The hardest thing is that no one knows about his love, not even the lady. He wishes that Amour and Pité would help him, but this seems impossible since the lady cannot send to him without damaging her honor, and he cannot approach her for fear of a rebuff which he could not endure. Then he muses that Alcyone found out what she wanted to know about Seys by praying to Juno, who sent her a vision of Seys by way of the God of Sleep and his son, Morpheus. If only, says the lover, Morpheus would appear to his lady five or six times and tell her how he is dying for her, then he would give Morpheus a cap and a feather-bed. In this hope the lover resolves to placate Morpheus, Amours, Dous Penser, and Bon Espoir, so that he will wear the "green hat" of happiness. If Morpheus does help him, he goes on, he will not trade his position for the crown of France or England; he will have a greater victory and more happiness than Pygmalion had with his statue. He concludes the complaint by bragging that all hundred of the rhymes he has used are different.

The poet verifies that there are indeed no rhymes repeated, then washes and dresses and goes to the house from which the voice came. There he finds in a large company a young lord, who "seemed to be the son of a king or the born sovereign lord of the land." The narrator falls on his knees in order to attract the lord's attention, and he is lifted to his feet by the great man, who courteously asks him why he is there. The poet gives his heart to the lord "ligement abandonez," and follows him into a beautiful garden to a fountain. No animals stand around because the statue

113

of Narcissus, which is there on a great pillar of ivory, is so lifelike that it scares them away. On the marble of the fountain are engraved a number of figures from the Troy story, and in the center is a twelve-headed serpent which spouts water. The lord tells the narrator that the fountain was formerly frequented by Jupiter, Venus, and Cupid, and that whoever drinks its water will be made amorous, whence it is called the "fonteinne amoreuse." He invites the poet to drink, but the poet declines because he feels amorous enough already. For a similar reason the lord himself refuses, confessing that he desperately loves a lady who does not know about his love. He does not dare tell her and now he must go away. He asks his new friend to write a complaint suitable to the occasion, and is surprised to be given his own complaint which the narrator had transcribed earlier.

The lord now falls asleep quite suddenly in his companion's lap. The narrator covers him, then goes to sleep also and has a long dream (ll. 1569-2526). In the dream two ladies appear, one carrying an apple of gold. She tells the lord that his worries are over, for she wills that he should obtain mercy and his liking. The lady, who identifies herself as Venus, then explains the apple she carries by telling the story of the marriage of Peleus, the apple of Discord, and the judgment of Paris. She recounts the legend to show her great *puissance*, which, she complains, the young lord has not recognized: he has not prayed to her, sacrificed bull, beef, or heifer, nor offered oil or incense. Nevertheless she will help him, she says; and she presents to him his beloved, whom she has brought with her.

The beloved comforts the lord in the twenty-stanza "Comfort de l'amant et de la dame" (ll. 2207-2526). She tells him that they should exchange hearts since Venus wishes it. Then, though he has to go away, he will have her heart to comfort him and she will have his. She instructs him further to remember what Venus did for Jupiter and Danaë and to rely on that goddess rather than fickle Fortune. Also, he should not worry because he is to be imprisoned and unable to seek glory, for she would rather have him healthy than a hero. She closes by admonishing him not to blame her for impropriety in coming to him, for Venus brought her. The lady then kisses her lover a hundred times and exchanges her ruby ring for a diamond of his. When the ladies have left, the two men awaken to find the ruby on the lord's finger.

After the lord expresses a desire to build a temple to Venus and another to Morpheus, and goes on to talk about the wedding feast which Venus had described, the men come to realize that they have had the same dream. The poet notes the precedent of the *Istoire des Romains*, which tells of a hundred senators having the same dream. The lover now becoming downcast because the lady has gone, the poet braces him up by recalling to him the ring, the kisses, and the fact that Venus has promised to help him. The final hundred lines (2745-2848) are occupied with realistic detail. A *chevalier* comes to tell the lord that they have spent half the day by the fountain and that the food spoils, so they go to Mass and dinner. Next day the narrator accompanies his noble friend to the port from which he will sail. The lord embarks on the fourth day, after having sung a *rondel* and given the narrator some jewels, "Truly more than were proper for me."

There is an obvious relationship between *Remede de Fortune* and *Fonteinne amoreuse* in the form and narrative function of the complaints, in the pattern of complaint and consolation, in the female deities who solve the lover's problem as a result of his petition, and in numerous details such as the attendance at Mass toward the end of each poem. These parallels showing how Machaut utilized his poem of twenty years before are impressive, but the analogies between the later Machaut poem and Chaucer's *Duchess* are even more striking, and they are particularly interesting because of the vivid contrast of the results.

The line-for-line indebtedness of the *Duchess* to the *Fonteinne amoreuse* is not great, being limited to the Seys and Alcyone legend and its narrative setting.[11] There are also general congruencies between Chaucer's and Machaut's version of this *exemplum*. Chaucer tells the story for the same overt reason that

115

Machaut's lover does, to exemplify the power of Morpheus, and as a result both poets emphasize the middle of Ovid's narrative. Seys' shipwreck at the beginning of Ovid's story and the metamorphosis of Seys and his wife into birds at the end, very important in the Latin version, are briefly treated by Machaut and nearly excised by Chaucer. But the relationship to Chaucer's *exemplum* is of limited importance in comparison with the relationship of Chaucer's elegy—i.e., the part during which the Black Knight is on the scene—to Machaut's whole poem.

The general congruency between the *Fonteinne amoreuse* and the elegy of the *Duchess* have been discussed in part in an article by Anna T. Kitchel.[12] She concludes simply that "Both poems consist essentially of confidences between two men; in each case moreover we have a poet confided in by a forlorn lover of royal birth."[13] Actually, the parallel extends quite a bit further. The similarity—in real life and in poetic representation—between the triangles of characters who are the main actors in the poems is most striking. Both Machaut and Chaucer depict a distraught lordly lover, who, bewailing his separation from his lady, is comforted by a poet-stranger. Machaut's poem is designed to palliate the distress of his young patron, Jean, Duc de Berry (third son of Jean II, King of France), on his enforced departure for England. In the *Duchess* Chaucer attempts to comfort an equally high-born young ducal patron also named John (third son of Edward III, King of England) on a distressing occasion of equal historicity. In each poem the patrons appear as anonymous courtly lovers, but the works equally provide quite definite identifications of the dukes in question (with a series of puns in the *Duchess* and an anagram in *Fonteinne*). The lady in Machaut's poem, like the lady in Chaucer's, evidently was the Duke's wife in real life, but is portrayed poetically as a courtly mistress.

Both poets, no doubt contrary to the historical facts, appear within the poems as having been unacquainted personally with the royal lovers previous to the events of the poem. The circumstances of the meetings of the poets with the noblemen occur (in the poems) as a result of very similar fortuitous events: both poets overhear lovers' complaints, set-pieces purportedly composed by the lovers. Each poet assumes a *persona* in the poem which is not wholly flattering, and each depicts himself as a frustrated lover who is willing to listen at length to, and to sympathize with, the troubles of the noblemen whose affairs provide the poetic subjects.

Of the numerous relationships of the *Duchess* to individual *dits amoreux*, its relationship to the *Fonteinne amoreuse* is the most fundamental. Most aspects of the Black Knight's complaints and story have counterparts in *Behaingne*; the pattern and details of the long prologue are extensively indebted to the *Roman de la Rose*; and the dream frame is directly based on Froissart's *Paradys d'Amours*. But the similarity of the basic narrative patterns of complaint and comfort, and of the manner in which almost identical real-life relationships of very comparable characters are presented poetically, argues that the influence of *Fonteinne amoreuse* on the *Duchess* is the most important of all.

The story which I set out to tell of the development of the *dit amoreux* from Guillaume de Lorris' poem to the *Book of the Duchess* is not entirely told. Froissart's *Paradys d'Amours*, which makes an important contribution, needs to be taken up, and other *dits* which have formerly been considered as sources must be reckoned with. But the rest of this story is somewhat anticlimactic, since its note is generally negative: the dream frame is not a constant or essential feature of the *dit amoreux*, and the other "sources" were probably written later than the *Duchess*. From another standpoint, though, the next two chapters have considerable interest, for they continue the history of the *dits* of complaint-and-consolation which has been begun in this chapter, and they show that Chaucer not only used the French poets as models, but also in turn provided a model for them.

CHAPTER VII

FROISSART'S POEMS OF COMPLAINT AND COMFORT

Jean Froissart was born, probably in 1337[1], in the town of Valenciennes in Hainault, the home province also of Queen Philippa of England — Edward III's wife and the mother of his twelve children. Jean as a young man must have been attached to some princely household in his own country, but there is no surviving record of this. At the age of twenty-four Froissart went "oultre la mer" to England.[2] His biographer thinks it is likely that he "crossed the channel with some of the many hostages who were then proceeding to England in execution of the terms of the Treaty of Brétigny,"[3] the unhappy time in the Duc de Berry's life which Machaut dramatized in the *Fonteinne amoreuse*. The treaty, however, did not supply Froissart's reason for going overseas. If one reads his *Espinette amoreuse* as autobiography, it appears that disappointment in love provided the incentive. But it seems probable that he had still other quite practical reasons for doing so, for soon after he presented himself at the English court in 1361, he became court chronicler and secretary to his countrywoman, the Queen; and he was associated with the court, with a couple of interruptions, till the Queen's death in August 1369, the month before Blanche of Lancaster died.

While in England Froissart was at the center of court life. He helped to celebrate the birth of the future Richard II in 1367. In 1368 he accompanied the Duke of Clarence on his journey to marry daughter of the Duke of Milan, and he acted virtually as official *trouvère* for the wedding. Since the Queen died while Jean was in Italy, Jean did not return to England with the Duke. Indeed, he was not again there till thirty-five years later when he presented Richard II an elaborate manuscript of his poetry. In the long meanwhile Froissart joined the clergy, enjoyed the patronage of such prominent courtiers as Wenceslaus of Brabant (son of Machaut's patron, Jean of Bohemia) and Guy of Blois, and was continuously busy with his chronicling. Jean returned to France in 1395 after a three-month visit in England, and he lived till sometime after 1404; his life span thus embraced Chaucer's with a few years to spare at each end.

Largely because of the importance of his *Chronicles*, the poetry of Froissart has not suffered neglect like that of his predecessor, Machaut. Kervyn de Lettenhove and F. S. Shears in particular have dealt with the poems in their biographical studies of Froissart, and as recently as 1946 B. J. Whiting published a survey of the poetry.[4] As these scholars have noted, the form and narrative of his poetry, particularly of his love narratives, is largely derived from the work of Machaut. Since most of the narratives were written after the *Book of the Duchess*, only three will be considered in detail here, two which have been seen as sources for the *Duchess*, and a third for which Chaucer's poem is a probable source. All three—the *Paradys d'Amours*, the *Espinette amoreuse*, and the *Dit dou bleu chevalier*—have the complaint-and-consolation form which originated with Machaut.

The personal and poetic relationship of Froissart to Chaucer is especially interesting. Though neither poet mentions an acquaintanceship with the other,[5] it can hardly be doubted that they were on familiar terms in the long period in the 1360's when they served together at the English court, especially since Chaucer's wife was probably a compatriot of Froissart's. The interrelationships between the work of Chaucer, Froissart, and Machaut, moreover, which show up in a detailed study of the *Duchess*, the *Paradys d'Amours*, *Remede de Fortune*, and *Fon-*

119

teinne amoreuse, strengthen the temptation which Whiting felt on a more cursory examination "to conjecture that the slightly older and more experienced youth from Hainault introduced the English boy to Machaut's poetry as well as his own."[6] One might mention too that as Chaucer wrote an elegy for his patroness, the Duchess, so Froissart wrote a *lay* lamenting his English sponsor, the Queen. Jean also commemorated Blanche's death in a few poignant lines in the *Joli buisson de jonece* (1373).[7]

Chaucer's major borrowing from Froissart's poetry is from the *Paradys d'Amours*, the main source for the dream frame of the *Duchess*. It has not always been accepted that Chaucer was the borrower, for Froissart's poem has a fourline sequence whose content seems dependent on his *Meliador*,[8] a romance which was not begun till after 1373, and not finished till after 1383.[9] This apparent dependence caused several scholars, including Skeat,[10] to assert that the similarities between the *Paradys* and the *Duchess* were due to Froissart's use of Chaucer's work. Other scholars believed, despite the reference to *Meliador*, that the weight of evidence overwhelmingly favors the priority of Froissart's poem;[11] and Professor Kittredge's article on this subject postulating a later insertion of the lines in question in the *Paradys* led to the present general accord that Froissart's poem antedates Chaucer's.[12] It is probably the first of his long poems.[13]

The narrative of the *Paradys* has extensive similarities to Machaut's *Remede de Fortune*. In both poems the lovers, while visiting garden spots, find occasion to make formal complaints (in the same strophic forms) attacking Amour. In each case the complaint, followed by a swoon, provokes the appearance of Esperance, whom Amant regards with half-open eyes. In both poems the lovers ask for and receive explanations of the functions of the figures who appear to them; in both Esperance agrees to stay with the Amant forever afterward.[14] The conclusions of the poems are similar in that the Amants, having been provided with courage to approach their ladies, are accepted as lovers. There is perhaps a subtler similarity in the personalities of the ladies in

120

question; both are practical, demanding, and quite apt at repartee. A further parallel is found between the slightly abbreviated tableau of intercalated lyrics of the *Paradys*—one each of five types plus two rondelets—and the nine lyrics of separate kinds in *Remede de Fortune.*

As in *Remede de Fortune,* the first-person narrator of the *Paradys d'Amours* is referred to as *Amant* in the text. Two important personifications in the poem, Jalousie and Plaisance, bear significances which differ so greatly from their present-day meanings as to be quite misleading. The editor defines Plaisance as "la personfication de la première sensation de bien-être, qu'-éprove un cœur frappé par les charmes d'une femme," and Jalousie as "irritation, mécontentement, désenchantement; c'est la contraire de plaisance, satisfaction intérieure."[15] *Paradys* has 1723 lines, less than half the number of *Remede de Fortune.*

The narrator opens the poem marvelling that he lives when he lies awake all the time with melancholy binding his heart [the first lines of the Duchess are nearly identical]. Not long ago, he continues, he did get some relief when he prayed to Morpheus, Juno, and Oleus to help him sleep. After he offered a gold ring to Juno, she had the God of Sleep send Enclimpostair to him, with the result that he slept with marvellous *pensées.* In his sleep it seems that he is sitting in a lovely wood with the nightingale singing such songs that he who heard them, though he had never loved before, would have to love. While sitting there love pains torment him, and he makes a *complainte* of eight sixteen-line stanzas to Amour (ll. 75-202). He laments that though Amour accepted his service and promised him mercy, his lady still gives him such hard looks that he knows she would rather have him in the grave than have to look at him. Calling Amour a traitor, he says he will dishonor him when he can, and he curses Plaisance because she made him give all to a lady who now makes him languish.

Amant swoons, but the sound of the branches rustling comes through to him after a while, and he looks up to see two well-dressed ladies advancing toward him. One says, "At him! At him! He came into the arbor that our lord made with his own hands, and then he spoke evil of him." Quickly falling to his knees, Amant begs forgiveness, and eventually mollifies them. He asks one of the ladies to tell him about their lord and about themselves. She answers (ll. 324 ff.) that she is Plaisance, the one who held the door when he gave homage to their master, and the other lady is Esperance. She recalls to Amant that Amour did not stipulate when he would obtain mercy, and that she cannot stay with him if Jalousie puts him out of his senses. A lover ought to be all patience and obedience with his lady, and a lady ought not to grant him grace at the first assault. Then Plaisance summarizes her own powers. She makes bodies appear gracious and pretty to lovers, so that each thinks his love has no equal. Such impressions cause Cupid's arrows to enter their hearts just as Achilles was stricken simply by looking at Polixena, and Neptune by seeing Leucothea, and Leander by seeing Hero.

When Amant asks if Plaisance can tell him when to expect mercy, Plaisance responds that he is likely to perish because of his impatience, and she asks Esperance to straighten him out (ll. 609 ff.). Esperance inquires if he has not drunk of Jalousie's beverage since the time he gave homage to Amour. Tell the truth, she admonishes him, for false confession leads to false absolution. He answers that "by St. Francis" he has been in so much pain that he cannot tell the truth. Esperance nevertheless agrees to be his advocate, and tells him to remember her always, whether he is on foot or horseback. When he asks for her, she promises, she will come with clenched fist to help him against Jalousie, and she will bring Franchise, Pité, Humilité, and several other helpers. "I am Esperance," she declares, "who weighs little when carried, and I fit into a small place; but my power is worth the gold of many cities." Esperance having concluded her lecture, she and Plaisance agree to show Amant around the grounds of Amour. Amant sings a *rondelet* as they go along, and they pass several figures who are engaged in the hunt of love.

122

Doulc Penser and Beau Semblant are holding hunting dogs, and Doulc Regard sounds the horn. Plaisance explains that Amour follows the hunt at this time of year without resting. The promenaders next pass by a *carole* in which figures from classical legend and medieval romance are engaged: Troilus, Paris, Percival, Tristan and Iseult, Galahad, Yvain, Echo, Hero, and Medea.

They eventually come to the pavilion of Amour, where Amant on the advice of Plaisance presents a *lay* to the king (ll. 1079-1354). In this lyric he claims that the lifeless statue of Pygmalion is the true figure of his love, which has enclosed him in the valley where Melampus bewailed his master, Actaeon. He compares his suffering to that of Tantalus, Achilles, Jason, Tristan, and Paris. Amour, impressed by Amant's sincerity, promises him such guerdon as true lovers deserve; but he warns that the lady is in his protection also, and if Desir sets Amant afire, Amour cannot save him from death. Now Amant, Esperance, and Plaisance go off singing a *virelay* and enter a meadow enclosed with rose bushes, lily plants, and columbines, where the nightingales sing very prettily. Amant is ecstatic when he finds his lady there; he kneels before her and, following the command of Amour, asks for grace. She inquires what he would have, over and beyond her showing him a pleasant countenance, and he requests that she hold him now and always as her loyal servant. After some banter, she accedes, but she warns that she is not foolish, that if he does not do his duty she will take everything back. They then sit down with Plaisance, Beauté, Franchise, Gaie Vie, Manière, Sens, Attemprance, Cremeur, Avis, and Pourveance beside them. While she makes him a chaplet of daisies, he sings perhaps the most famous of Froissart's balades, which has the refrain, "Above all I love the daisy" (*margarite*). Afterwards the lady takes the chaplet she had made, kisses it, has him kiss it, and places it on his head.

Her look is so delightful that Plaisance seems to touch Amant, causing him to tremble and wake up. When he finds himself in his own bed, he thanks Morpheus for the dream in which there was nothing false; he thanks Orpheus for showing him the art of singing; and he thanks Iris, the messenger of the God of Sleep,[16] for her help. Thus, concludes the poet, was I once ravished into the amorous paradise.

Despite the close relationship of *Remede de Fortune* to *Paradys d'Amours*, Chaucer employs these poems in wholly distinct parts of the *Duchess*. To *Remede de Fortune* Chaucer's chief debt is for the complaint against fortune and miscellaneous matters in the elegy proper, and to *Paradys d'Amours* it is for the frame story.[17] Chaucer's use of *Paradys d'Amours* in the frame of the dream— the parts before the poet goes to sleep and after he wakes up— and his failure to use it any place within the dream certainly indicate that he was conscious of the frame as a separate division of the poem and of the *Paradys* as the source for that part. Other poems are important sources for the Seys and Alcyone, which is in the frame; but before and after this *exemplum*, up till the dream, and in the last fourteen lines of the work, after the dreamer awakens, lines borrowed from the *Paradys* predominate.[18] Narrative parallels in the frame go along with the verbal correspondences. In both the *Paradys* and the *Duchess* the poet is troubled with insomnia and melancholy thoughts, which cause and ensue from his sleeplessness; the thoughts are occasioned by the poet's love and his frustration in pursuit of his love. Each poet prays for sleep to Juno and Morpheus, offering gifts; he thereupon goes to sleep, and is subsequently convinced that he would not have slept if it had not been for these prayers. Each has a dream which he believes is meaningful, and is awakened by a happening in the dream (in the respective cases, a touch from Plaisance and the sounding of a clock tower). Each poet, as soon as he wakes up, consciously notes that he is in his own bed, and each closes on a professional note with a statement about the poetic material which the dream has provided.

Froissart's decision to put the narrative of the *Paradys* within a dream, and Chaucer's decision to follow him, was clearly a

124

matter of the poet's choice. Despite the common assumption of critics, dream poems did not constitute a separate category of love narratives.[19] Of the works of Machaut which Froissart and Chaucer used as models for the *Paradys* and the *Duchess*, only *Fonteinne amoreuse* has a dream, and it occupies but a third of the work. Of the other *dits* already studied, the majority do not have a dream frame comparable to that of the *Roman de la Rose*. The only ones which do are the *Fablel dou Dieu d'Amours*, the *Panthère d'Amours*, the *Messe des oisiaus*, and Machaut's *Dit dou Vergier*.

Even when the poet chose to place his story within a vision, the vision apparatus could be quite variable. Several of Watriquet de Couvin's works exemplify the range of machinery available to the trouvère for visions with all kinds of subjects. His *Mireoirs as dames* exemplifies the waking vision: the poet thinks so hard that he is entranced, and in his thoughts Aventure shows him true beauty. The vision of the *Dis de l'Arbre Royal*, an allegory designed to praise Charles le Bel and his family, occurs in a real dream that has a notable resemblance to the dreams of the *Paradys d'Amours* and the *Duchess* in that it occurs in immediate answer to a prayer which the poet makes while lying in his bed. In the *Dis de la Fontaine d'Amours* (discussed in Chapter III) the vision provides an interesting variation on the dream framework: of the two parts of the vision, one occurs before the poet sleeps and the other while he is sleeping. The circumstances of the vision of the *Dis des .iiii. sièges* are still more unusual. The dream takes place while the narrator is sleeping with his beloved, an unpropitious time it would seem for the glimpse of the Christian Heaven which he is granted. Furthermore, without explanation the bedfellow disappears between the beginning and end of the dream. The *Tournois des dames* (also discussed in Chapter III), like *Mireoirs as dames*, is not really a dream vision. But while the latter vision takes place in a waking trance, in the *Tournois* the vision of the parables of Verité occurs between waking and sleeping. In the *Dis des trois vertus* the poet dreams that Loyalty, Charity, and Truth are in power at Rome, but it turns out to be an hallucinating dream, in contrast to the other poems of Watriquet discussed here which all purport to present views of transcendent truth. Finally, the *Dis de l'escharbote* employs quite straightforwardly the most familiar of dream-vision frames: springtime setting, a walk to a garden by a poet overjoyed at the return of flowers and birds, and a nap there in which he has a marvellous dream.

The situations underlying these seven visions of Watriquet, then, very considerably. Two visions do not occur in dreams, but rather in trancelike states. One vision begins before the dream begins, one vision is hallucinatory, one occurs in answer to a prayer, and one comes upon the poet when he is in bed with his beloved. The settings are also variable. Two of them begin in garden spots, three while the poet is in his own bed, one in a tower, and the other when the poet is sitting in his chamber. Nor is the season or hour of the day fixed. Springtime is associated with a number of these visions, but in others is not specified. The hour, when mentioned, seems to have no special significance.[20] Thus Watriquet uses a considerable assortment of vision situations. Though the components of these situations are mostly conventional, he combines them in an apparently arbitrary fashion, occasionally adding idiosyncratic twists.

Most of the dream machinery of the *Duchess*, as the foregoing analysis shows, finds precedent in Watriquet's work as well as in the direct source, Froissart's *Paradys*. This fact simply serves to demonstrate that there was a fund of materials for poetic visions which the poet of the day could draw upon. But Watriquet's visions also show that no feature was absolutely necessary: neither springtime, birds, a garden, a fountain, a prayer, a bed, a guide, divine revelation, nor a dream. Thus Chaucer was free to put his story in a dream or not, and to select conventional details as suited his artistic purpose. The conventions provided important tools, but they did not control.

In addition to his *Paradys d'Amours*, Froissart's *Espinette amoreuse* has been suggested as a source for details of Chaucer's *Duchess* by Sypherd and by J. Burke Severs.[21] But the correspondences they find are so faint as to be worthless as evidence of Chaucer's use of the poem. As a matter of fact, since Froissart was in England with Chaucer up till 1368 the very lack of significant correspondences between the *Duchess* and the *Espinette* rather supports an hypothesis that Froissart dit not write his poem till after his return to Hainault. Such an hypothesis agrees with the supposition of the poem's most recent editor, though it damages the correlation of the events of the work with the poet's biography.[22]

Auguste Scheler calls the *Espinette amoreuse* "the best-known, the most cited and also the most attractive of Froissart's poetic compositions".[23] A great part of such praise seems to be based on the ostensibly autobiographical nature of the story: a veneer of personification, mythological allusion, and commonplaces of the idealized love story barely covers the description of realistic situations and events. In this regard the *Espinette* is related to Machaut's *Voir Dit*. The poem is also like *Remede de Fortune* and *Fonteinne amoreuse* in various matters of detail, in its patterns of complaint and comfort, and in the fact that its 4192 lines contain fourteen lyric set-pieces, including a complaint with a hundred different rhymes and a "Comfort de la dame", both in the sixteen-line stanzas employed by Machaut.

The poet introduces his subject with a prologue in which he relates some youthful experiences (ll. 1-338). Amour, he says, took him into his service even before he had given up the games which children under twelve play. He then digresses to describe fifty-two ways in which he used to pass his time, such as playing in brooks with feathers as boats, chasing butterflies and putting them on a string, and using a stick to make a horse named Grisel. As he got older, he had to learn Latin, and he was beaten if he did not do his lesson. He would also get beaten by his fellows sometimes in wrestling, and would go home with his clothes torn to get beaten again. But he could not be restrained,

127

for he had a light heart. Nature and Amour nurtured him; in summer Amour led him to delight in violets, roses, and peonies; and in winter he read romances and learned the proprieties of love and its worth.

One day in May, shortly after sunrise, three ladies and a young man approach the poet. The young man, who is Mercury, asks him to review the Judgment of Paris. The poet protests, but when Mercury insists, he confirms Paris' original judgment and Venus promises him a heart "gai, joli et amoreus" all his life, and a lady to love. A few days after this the poet does indeed meet a lady with whom he falls in love. She is reading the romance of *Cléomadès*, and they subsequently read together this romance and others. By various means he tries to indicate to her his love: he writes her a *balade* which she ignores; he tries to get amorous at a *carole* but she tells him not to spoil the fun; and then he sends a *balade* by the lady's *confidante* asking for the "gracieus don de merci" but the lady merely comments to her friend that he is asking for a lot. Then one day the confidante informs the poet that the marriage of the lady is being considered. He takes to bed and delivers an eight-hundred line complaint (1555-2354) in which he likens his plight to that of Apollo and Daphne, and at length he decides that it would be best to die. But after three and a half months he is once more ambulatory and sets off overseas for his health. Aboard ship he ignores a storm in which the vessel nearly founders, and he recites *rondels* about his lady while admiring constantly a mirror of hers which the confidante had given him. One night, after arriving at his destination, he dreams that he sees his lady in the mirror combing her hair. She recites to him a 240-line poem of comfort (ll. 2752-2991) avowing her love for him—as strong as the love of Yseult, Guinevere, or Hero—and promising him her love if he will be patient a little longer.

The lady disappears (l. 2991) and the poet awakens with the feeling that the dream lied to him, but he thanks Morpheus nevertheless for having shown him his beloved. Subsequently, though he continues to enjoy himself in the country he is visiting (presumably England), he becomes increasingly anxious about the lady, and finally seeks and secures from the woman whom he is serving (presumably Queen Philippa) permission to depart. Back home he is encouraged first by his lady's friend, then by the lady herself. The three get together often, sometimes in a room with a flowered carpet which he calls the "Vregier de la Droite Dame." The affair is proceeding very well when suddenly the confidante dies, which makes communication between the pair difficult. The poet nevertheless encounters the lady one day in a garden where she is enjoying herself with other people, and she makes him a chaplet of flowers. When she has him kiss it, his lips are wounded by two thorns. Another time, on the first of May, the poet picnics with her and she accepts him for her own. Unfortunately Male Bouche finds out about this and the lady tells the poet she cannot be seen with him. One day much later he sees her alone and asks to sit with her, but she declines. She pulls his hair as he passes by, however, an amorous gesture as he interprets it. The poet now closes with a *lay* and with an anagram revealing his and his lady's names—*Jehan Froissart* and a *Margherite* of an uncertain last name.

Several other poems of Froissart are in the tradition of the *dit amoreux*. The *Prison amoreuse* (3,899 lines plus several long prose letters), which has many correspondences with Machaut's *Voir Dit*, was written to comfort Wenceslas of Brabant in his imprisonment in 1371-72. In the *Joli buisson de jonece*, a long (5,439 lines) narrative in which the poet is again the central figure, Lady Philosophy appears to him outside a dream and Venus within it. The *Joli mois de May* (464 lines) consists mostly of description of the narrator's beloved. And the *Dit dou bleu chevalier* is another poem of complaint and comfort. All of these were probably written after the *Espinette amoreuse*,[24] and therefore could not have influenced the *Duchess*. Nevertheless it seems quite clear that there is a relationship between Chaucer's poem and the *Bleu chevalier*, so that some consideration of that poem is in order.

129

The correspondences in diction between the two poems are not remarkable, but the narratives are alike on many points. In both the narrators overhear knights who are dressed from head to toe in a single color that is symbolical of their present conditions. Each narrator listens unobserved to the knight's complaint and sees that he is violently affected by his grief, this fact leading the narrator to make himself known to the knight. Each cautions the knight against suicide, citing classical examples of lovers who killed themselves for their loves and the example of Socrates who was not affected by the whims of Fortune. Both knights reject the consolation offered with counter-arguments of their own, though both are courteous and apparently grateful to their comforters. As a summary should help to demonstrate, these parallels are not attributable to the poems of Machaut which also influenced the *Bleu chevalier*. The poem, 504 lines in length, is written throughout in the four-line strophes of Machaut's *Behaingne*.

Walking toward a wood one day near the end of April, begins the poet, he catches sight of a knight, dressed all in blue (the blue of fidelity, it must be assumed). The knight acts strangely and inconsistently, first singing a chanson happily, then sitting by a tree (like Chaucer's Knight) making "grans regrés,/ Cris, plours et plains et pluiseurs aultres lés" (ll. 45-46). Secreting himself close to the Knight in order to hear what he is saying, the narrator listens to a forty-line complaint in which the knight laments that he has been taken from everything that he loves (ll. 71-112). But again he becomes happy thinking that his lady is so courteous and loyal that she will not act in a proud manner when he returns, and still again he becomes sad, so affected that the narrator thinks he is dead. At this point the narrator goes up and bathes the Blue Knight's face with spring water, and when the knight looks up the two men recognize each other. The narrator is abashed because of the high rank of the knight, and he wishes to leave, but the knight tells him to feel welcome.

The narrator and the Blue Knight now have a conversation

about his sorrows. Do not be like Piramus and Leander, says the narrator, who killed themselves for their loves, but be like Socrates who disdained Fortune. The knight, however, laments that he is held here like a bird and that all of his youth will be lost. His companion reminds him that Tristan, Lancelot, Yvain, and Perceval could not spend much time beside their ladies but were loved the more by them for their exploits; but the knight points out that his case is not comparable to that of the Arthurian knights, since he is unable to go any place and accomplish heroic exploits. He wishes that he could come to the end of "ceste voie" (l. 361) or ransom himself, or that he could go to his lady or she come to him. In reply the narrator simply encourages the knight again to be like Socrates in enduring the blows of Fortune. Professing now to be consoled, the knight requests that his companion write a poem about this experience. The poet asks the lady's name, but the knight says that it would lessen his honor to reveal it. The knight then leaves and the poet writes the *dit*, expressing the hope that Amour will comfort worthy lovers.

The *Bleu chevalier* has been ignored by most critics, and the occasion of its composition left in the dark. Whiting misrepresents the story considerably in his summary, not recognizing that the poem belongs to prison literature. His guess that the work was written "for one of Froissart's noble friends or patrons"[25] nevertheless seems safe, for the awed reaction of the narrator in the poem upon recognizing the knight, and the clear intimation that the lady has a real-life name—i.e., is not fictional—indicate that the *Bleu chevalier* is an occasional piece. The subject of the work could have been the Duc de Berry, who laments in Machaut's *Fonteinne amoreuse* that he will waste his youth in prison, unable to acquire honor (ll. 407-416). Froissart and the Duke were in England together while the Duke was hostage there. The subject might also have been Wenceslas of Brabant, for whom Froissart wrote his *Prison amoreuse* while Wenceslas was a prisoner of war in 1371-73. But either identification presents problems; a third alternative seems to be needed, which I am not prepared to offer. The assumption here, that the *Bleu chevalier* followed the *Duchess*, would rule out the first possibility. This assumption is supported by Froissart's failure to name his *Bleu chevalier* in his list of works in the *Joli buisson de jonece* (1373).

The precedence of the *Duchess* is also supported by internal evidence, particularly by the passage in which Socrates is presented as an example of fortitude. The dreamer tells the Black Knight in the *Duchess*:

> "Remembre yow of Socrates,
> For he ne counted nat thre strees
> Of noght that Fortune koude doo." (ll. 717-719)

Then he tells the knight that he would be foolish to kill himself for sorrow over love as did Medea, Phyllis, Dido, Echo, and Samson. This passage evidently owes its inspiration to the *Roman de la Rose*, where Raison, having cited Echo as an example of immoderate grief, then mentions Socrates who did not give "une prune" for all the wheel of Fortune (ll. 5834-50). The correspondences between Chaucer's "three strees" and Jean de Meun's "prune" and between Chaucer's and Jean's use of Echo as a bad example indicate that Chaucer used the *Rose* directly for this passage. Had he employed Froissart's poem in addition, he probably would have used the examples of Piramus and Leander which Froissart made use of in the similar passage of the *Bleu chevalier*. For though Chaucer does add to lists of classical examples from his sources, he does not characteristically reject their examples. Furthermore, when Chaucer makes important use of another poem, he generally takes both language and narrative, as when—to cite the most relevant instance—he uses Froissart's *Paradys d'Amours* for the dream frame of the *Duchess*. On the other hand, Froissart's practice is to take the story and the form from others, but to use his own language and to make the *exempla* his own.[26] Thus the lack of significant parallels in language between the *Bleu chevalier* and the *Book of the Duchess*, coupled

132

with the pervasive narrative parallels, suggests that Chaucer was not the borrower.

My conclusion, then, is that there is an undoubted close relationship between the *Duchess* and the *Bleu chevalier*, and that in this case Froissart borrows from Chaucer. Just as Chaucer in the *Duchess* made important use of three Machaut poems and one of Froissart, so Froissart in the *Bleu chevalier* employs the same three Machaut narratives and Chaucer's *Duchess*. It is entirely possible that Froissart first obtained a copy of the *Duchess* from his and Chaucer's mutual friend, Richard Stury, who travelled from London to Brussels in early 1371 when Froissart was there.[27]

Froissart's three poems of complaint and comfort thus have three different relationships to the *Duchess*. The *Paradys d'Amours*, in all likelihood written while Chaucer and Froissart were in England together, is an important source of Chaucer's poem. The *Espinette amoreuse*, on the other hand, was probably written around 1370 after Froissart returned to the continent and before he had seen *Book of the Duchess*, so that it has no direct relationship to Chaucer's poem, though both works have the complaint-and-comfort narrative pattern derived from common sources. Finally, the *Bleu chevalier* was written some time after Froissart had read the *Book of the Duchess* and was strongly influenced by Chaucer's elegy. Though Chaucer's influence on his French contemporaries has not been previously demonstrated, in this case it seems most probable. The *Duchess* even more clearly provides a source for the *Songe vert* and two of Granson's complaints which have been seen previously as influential on Chaucer's work. A consideration of these poems occupies most of the next chapter, which concludes this study.

CHAPTER VIII

OTHER POEMS OF COMPLAINT AND COMFORT

Three other poems of complaint and comfort, which are obviously related to works taken up in the last two chapters, have been treated as sources for the central situation of the *Book of the Duchess*: the *Songe vert* and two of Granson's complaints. Several factors, however, suggest that these poems are descendants of Chaucer's work rather than antecedents. In the first place, the language and situation of the parts of the *Duchess* in question are mostly accounted for by other poems which undoubtedly were written before 1369. Secondly, the dating of these supposed sources before the *Duchess* is questionable, even unlikely. Finally, the interrelationships of these works with the *Duchess* and with the various poems of complaint and comfort indicate the priority of Chaucer's poem.

   To facilitate discussion, it will be helpful to look again at the dramatic situation which provides the setting for Chaucer's elegy, and to review the role of Machaut's narratives in this part. In the *Duchess* after the dreamer catches sight of the Black Knight, he listens to his eleven-line "maner song," watches him almost swoon, then walks up to him. The knight for a long time does not notice the dreamer standing there with his hat respectfully in his hands, but when he does he apologizes. The two exchange declarations that they have not been offended, either by being overlooked or intruded upon. When the knight admits that he is not really interested in the hunt, the dreamer responds that he suspected as much from his appearance, and that he would like to do something to help him. He could not be helped by all the remedies of Ovid, the knight answers; even Death proves himself his enemy by always fleeing from him. His laughter and good times, he continues, have all been turned to weeping by Fortune, who checkmated him by stealing his "fers". The dreamer in response tells him that he must adopt the stolidity of Socrates in the face of Fortune, for it would do him no more good to kill himself than it did Dido or Phyllis. To this the knight answers that he has lost more than the dreamer realizes, and says that he will tell about it if he will listen with all his "wyt". He then recites his tragic experience.

Machaut's *Behaingne* and *Fonteinne amoreuse* provide a number of analogues to the general situation of this section. In *Behaingne*, as in Chaucer's poem, the narrator eavesdrops in the woods on love complaints of knights, and the lady of *Behaingne* has lost her lover by death as has the Black Knight his beloved. In *Fonteinne amoreuse* the narrator overhears a formal complaint and offers comfort to the complainer; furthermore, the real-life counterparts of the poetic characters on stage in *Fonteinne* and the *Duchess* are remarkably analogous.

In addition to these general parallels, specific adaptations of Machaut's poems pervade the parts of the Duchess under consideration. *Behaingne* (ll. 193-200) and the *Third Motet* (ll. 1-8) account for most of the Black Knight's eleven-line complaint. The Black Knight's failing physical state is described in the terms with which Machaut tells about the failing physical state of the lady after she has told her story. The lady's failure to see the knight of *Behaingne* until he takes hold of her, and then her apologies to him for not returning his greeting, followed by his objections that no apology is needed, obviously provide the basis for the dreamer's first encounter with the Black Knight:

He sayde, "I prey the, be not wroth.
I herde the not, to seyn the soth,
Ne I sawgh the not, syr, trewely."

"A, goode sir, no fors," quod y,
"I am ryght sory yif I have ought
Destroubled yow out of your thought.
Foryive me, yif I have mystake."
"Yis, th'amendes is lyght to make,"
Quod he, "for ther lyeth noon therto;
There ys nothyng myssayd nor do."   (ll. 519-528)

"Certes, sire, pas ne vous entendi
Pour mon penser qui le me deffendi;
          Mais se j'ay fait
Riens ou il ait villenie ou meffait,
Vueilliez le moy pardonner, s'il vous plait."
Li chevaliers, sans faire plus de plait,
          Dist doucement:
"Dame, Il n'affiert ci nul pardonnement,
Car il n'y a meffait ne mautalent;
Mais je vous pri que vostre pensement
          Me vueilliez dire."   (ll. 70-80)

The dreamer's desire in the *Duchess* to help the knight and his
suggestion that the knight's telling his story might ease his heart
also find a counterpart in *Behaingne*, in the knight's statement
that if the lady will tell her story he will do all that he can to ease
her suffering. In her response that no one except God can assuage
her sorrow the Black Knight's protest is paralleled.

The long complaint which Chaucer's knight lodges against
Fortune is drawn from *Remede de Fortune* and from other works
of Machaut. The remarkable exchange between the Black
Knight and the dreamer following the discussion of Fortune, in
which the knight insists on the importance of the dreamer listening
very carefully, finds a source—though not an explanation—in
Behaingne:

"I telle the upon a condicioun
That thou shalt hooly, with al thy wyt,
Do thyn intent to herkene hit."
"Yis, syr." "Swere thy trouthe therto."
"Gladly." "Do thanne holde hereto!"

136

"I shal ryght blythely, so God me save,
Hooly with al the wit I have,
Here yow, as wel as I kan." (ll. 750-757)

There is nothing in the immediate context of Chaucer's poem to justify this nagging insistence of the knight that the dreamer be wholly attentive (which sounds very like Hamlet's importuning Horatio and Marcellus to "Swear!"). In *Behaingne* the knight has a specific reason for asking the lady to be attentive, for he thinks that she is too absorbed in her own trouble:

"... mais que vous m'escoutez,
Et que vo cuer de tristesse gettez,
Par quoy toute vostre entente mettez
        A moy oir."
"Certes, sire, po me puis resjoir.
Mais j'en feray mon pouoir, sans mentir." (ll. 253-258)

The Appendix shows in graph form how almost all of the language of Chaucer's elegy section (ll. 443-1313) has a close source in Machaut. Analysis shows further that nearly every facet of the situation and every step in the story also have analogues in the works of Machaut from which the verbal expression is drawn. This being the case, it would seem that a parallel in situation in another poem to the same parts of the *Duchess* should suggest that the other poem follows the *Duchess*, the details of Chaucer's poem already being in great part accounted for. Thus, when a critic comparing the *Duchess* and the *Songe vert* finds that "the situation, the characters, the relationships between the characters (their attitude toward each other, and the way in which they affect each other and seek to affect each other), the order and substance of the words they address to each other are all alike in the two poems,"[1] this critic is probably showing that the *Duchess* was a source for *Songe vert*, not vice versa. Nothing in the dating of *Songe vert* contradicts this probability, and there are several specific matters of internal evidence which support it. A summary of the French work will help to bring these points out.

137

The author of *Songe vert*[2] is unknown, but the dialect identifies him as a native of Ile-de-France or Picardy. The work has 1822 lines and exists in two manuscripts. The narrator, who is the central figure in the poem, begins by relating how one morning at daybreak—a long time after he was deprived of all joy by Fortune in the cursed year which had deprived many ladies and many knights of their loves—he arises, dresses himself in his *habit noir*, and goes out walking beside a river. As he is praying to God for an early death, he comes to a *vergier*, where the sun is resplendent on the grass, and the birds are happily singing "motez, chansonetes et lais," each according to his liking.

It upsets him mightily that *bestelettes* without reason can have such happiness. He sits beside a dry hedge of thorns, thinking of the great sorrow that Fortune has given him, and begins to bewail his lot aloud. Hearing the bell ring in the church where his beloved lies, like one out of his mind he staggers toward the river to drown himself, but he falls from weakness before he can get there. He realizes then that Death is completely against him, for it will neither come to him nor permit him to go to it. He is weak from lying awake many nights, so he goes to sleep there beside the river and is seized by a marvellous dream. In the dream (ll. 225 ff.) the Queen of Love appears and orders him to forget his sorrow. When he reproaches her for having deprived him of his only possible source of happiness, she responds that Fortune was responsible for the lady's death, and bids him to return to Amor's service. "Cursed be the day I serve you," he exclaims, but she recalls that he has vowed to serve, fear, believe, and obey her all his life. Over his protests, she promises to cause to love him the most beautiful lady that has been born since Nostre Dame, the fountain of honor and full of humility. She then bids him to think on the joys of loving.

The thought of these joys cause him to faint, but the Queen resuscitates him by washing his face with some water that Plaisance fetches from the river, and by feeding him an electuary brought by Desir. Now that he feels much better, the Queen

138

orders him to take off his black clothes. When he demurs, she reduces his resistance by showing him a vision of the lady. Desir and Bon Espoir by main force then strip him and reclothe him in green. The lover, finally subjected, swears eternal obedience to the Queen.

The lover now turns and sees a fleur-de-lis (l. 1020) so handsome that all the valley in which it grows seems lighted by it. The Queen of Love explains that this flower represents his new love, whom he will always call *Flor-que-tot-passe*. The erstwhile mourner thinks himself unworthy of such a paragon, but the Queen explains that the lady will love him by virtue of her humility. As the Queen prepares to leave, she enjoins her reformed subject to be loyal always lest the "beste envenimee" [slanderer?] harm them; and having blessed him, she takes him by the chin and kisses him goodbye, promising to return within three months. Loiauté and Plaisance also kiss him, and Bon Espoir and Desir take their leave, but Desir assures him that she will be right back. After the Queen and her retinue have departed (l. 1560), the lover climbs a high tree to get a better look at the fleur-de-lis and sees to his dismay a hideous thorn plant growing next to it [husband or rival?] In his rage he leaps out of the tree in order to tear up the ugly plant, and the fall awakens him. He is surprised to find that he really does have on a "robe vert", and the dry hedge beside which he went to sleep has become verdant. When he returns home, his servants, overjoyed to see him dressed in green, inform him that all his black garments have turned to green. He is thus forced to submit to serving Amor. The poet closes with the announcement that he is sending this poem to a worthy brother (*sister* in the second manuscript), one who knows the sorrows and joys of love.

Léopold Constans assumes that the reference to a cursed year "Que fu la grant mortalité" is "sans doute" an allusion to the Black Plague, which, having appeared in Provence in Novemver of 1347, arrived in Paris and the north of France in spring 1348.[3] He therefore dates the poem some time shortly after 1348. Ethel

Seaton, however, notes that such dating appears early for the manuscripts and that there were other years in the fourteenth century when ladies and knights lost many loved ones to the Black Death. She chooses the year 1393 when Richard's Queen Anne was a victim, and ascribes the *Songe vert* to Gower or Froissart.[4] One might also suggest the year 1369 when both Philippa and Blanche succumbed to the pestilence, and might even imagine that *Songe vert* is a sequel to the *Duchess*, written to encourage or justify John of Gaunt's marriage to Constance of Castile of to another eligible lady. But there are problems of detail in this solution too.[5] The main point to be made is that other years than 1348 suit the reference to the plague, and that the later dating indicated by other considerations is not in the least ruled out.

To date the *Songe vert* around 1348 would be to place it between Machaut's *Remede de Fortune* and *Fonteinne amoreuse*, and to see it as accounting for several isolated narrative components of *Fonteinne amoreuse* and *Paradys d'Amours*. For example, the introduction of the beloved in a dream by a deity of love is found in *Fonteinne amoreuse* and *Paradys d'Amours*, as well as in *Songe vert* (but not in *Remede de Fortune*). But in other respects these works of Machaut and Froissart are much more closely related to each other and to *Remede de Fortune* than they are to *Songe vert*, and *Songe vert* is more closely allied to the *Duchess* and the *Bleu chevalier*, the later complaint-and-comfort poems. If this kind of narrative developed in any coherent manner, it is necessary to date *Songe vert* after *Fonteinne amoreuse* (1360). Analysis of similarities in phrasing between the *Duchess* and *Songe vert*, moreover, seem conclusive in assigning the latter a later date than Chaucer's poem.

Severs, in his recent article on "The Sources of 'The Book of the Duches',"[6] chooses to ignore Miss Seaton's arguments for another dating for *Songe vert*, and, as Sypherd had long ago,[7] treats that poem as another source for Chaucer. He enumerates some striking parallels in expression between the two poems

140

where there are no comparable lines in other works.[8] In such cases, of course, if the dating is questionable then the line of borrowing is also questionable. What establishes this line are the other parallels that Severs cites, which "occur also in Machaut's *Jugement dou Roy de Behaingne,* usually in a form closer to Chaucer's lines."[9] It does not seem reasonable to imagine that both poets went back to Machaut for the same lines, which occur in the debate poem *Behaingne* in a rather different narrative context from *Songe vert* and the *Duchess,* while these latter poems provide much the same contexts for the lines. It is easier to imagine, indeed it is almost certain, that one of the poets wrenched the Machaut lines out of context to put into a complaint-and-comfort poem, that the other poet borrowed from the first borrower, and that the expression which is closest to Machaut (i.e., Chaucer's) indicates the poet who did the initial borrowing. If Machaut's *Behaingne* is the oldest, as it surely is (before 1342), then the line of borrowing goes from *Behaingne* to the *Duchess* to *Songe vert,* as the following parallel passages suggest:

"De nos deus cuers estoit si juste paire
Qu'onques ne fu l'un a l'autre contraire;
    Einsois estoient
Tuit d'un acort; une pensée avoient;
De volenté, de desir se sambloient;
Un bien, un mal, une joie sentoient
    Conjointement."   (*Behaingne,* 166-172)

"Oure hertes wern so evene a payre,
That never nas that oon contrayre
To that other, for no woo.
For sothe, ylyche they suffred thoo
Oo blysse, and eke oo sorwe bothe."   (*Duchess,* 1289-93)

"Si te comant a Dieu atant,
Que doint et a li et a toi
Tant de bien com jo vueil par moi,
Si qu'il vos tiegne chescun jor
En un cuer et en une amor."   (*Songe vert,* 1434-38)

The relationships of the italicized lines in the three passages may be particularly noted, in addition to the congruities of the complete passages.

A final indication of the priority of the *Duchess* is provided by one of the parallels cited by Severs which has no counterpart in Machaut. In both *Songe vert* and Chaucer's poem the bereft lover tells of seeking death unsuccessfully:

> The pure deth is so ful my foo
> That I wolde deye, hyt wolde not soo;
> For whan I folwe hyt, hit wol flee;
> I wolde have hym, hyt nyl nat me. (ll. 583-586)

> Et lors j'aperçui le debat
> Que la desleiaus Mort metoit,
> Quand vers moi venir ne voloit
> Ne sofrir que vers li alasse. (ll. 174-177)

But Severs (along with previous editors and commentators) did not note that these lines are simply versifications of a passage of the Apocalypse in which there is a vision of locusts whose "torment was as the torment of a scorpion" (ix. 5). In that dreadful time, to quote Chaucer's own literal translation of Apocalypse ix. 6 in the Parson's Tale,

> They shullen folwe deeth, and they shul nat fynde hym; and they shul desiren to dye, and deeth shal flee fro hem.[10]

Aside from the fact that throughout his work Chaucer makes great use of literary allusion and quotes extensively from other writings, particularly the Bible, and that the author of the *Songe vert* shows little tendency in this direction, the precedence of Chaucer's lines is indicated because they are closer to the language of the Bible than the French lines. The statement that death will *flee* (*fugiet*) occurs in both the *Duchess* and the Apocalypse, and there is no similar word in *Songe vert*. The line of borrowing, then, from older source (in this case, the Bible) to the *Duchess* to *Songe vert* again is indicated.

142

Taking into account the evidence for dating, the inter-relationships of the complaint-and-comfort poems, and the evidence supplied by similarities in expression between the two poems and other texts, there should be little question that *Songe vert* was written some time after the *Book of the Duchess*. In turn, it seems very likely that Oton de Granson's complaints followed *Songe vert*, since the narrative of the *Complainte de Saint Valentin* is obviously related to that work. In both poems the bereaved at the behest of a deity of love gives up his mourning and takes a new mistress. The well-developed narration of this incident in *Songe vert* and its sketchy appearance in Granson's poem argues for the former's precedence. In any event, other factors indicate that Granson's two complaints imitate, and are not imitated by, Chaucer's *Book of the Duchess*.

Chaucer adapted and translated some ballades and Valentine poetry of the Savoyard knight Granson, and in the *Complaint of Venus* (a work probably of the 1390's) the English poet calls him "flour of hem that make in Fraunce" (1. 82). Granson, born in the 1340's, was probably very near Chaucer's age; and he and Chaucer were no doubt in fairly close contact after Granson entered the service of John of Gaunt in 1374.[11] The relationship which they had before 1374 is problematical. It is known that Granson sailed with the English expeditionary force from Southampton against the Spanish in 1372. Haldeen Braddy surmises that he probably attended the marriage festivities of Lionel, Duke of Clarence, in May 1368, and that he might have met Chaucer there, who perhaps had joined Lionel in Italy.[12] It is necessary to envisage some such contact between the two poets if one is to maintain with Braddy that Granson's *Complainte de l'an nouvel* and *Complainte de Saint Valentin* influence the *Duchess*.

La Complainte de l'an nouvel que Gransson fist pour un chevalier qu'il escoutoit complaindre is composed of eight stanzas of the form used in the Monk's Tale. The poet, *par melancolie*, goes out into the wood one New Year's Eve and overhears a knight making a very bitter complaint. He castigates Amor, who hates him, his lady, who wishes his death, and his heart, which consents to the situation. But especially he blames his eyes which used to take such delight in seeing her, and now make him miserable when she forbids him the sight of her. The knight sighs deeply, and when the poet sees that he is about to begin his plaint once more, he goes forward to comfort him:

> Et quant son plaing recommencier vouloit,
> Je vins avant pour le reconforter,
> Et le gettay du penser qu'il avoit. (ll. 61-63)

As Piaget notes, this poem of Granson is accompanied in one manuscript by a strophe-by-strophe refutation written by a certain *Lesparra*. This poet has been identified with Florimont the lord of Lesparra, who was a captive in Spain with Sir Oton. Piaget suggests that these two captives could have shared the same prison and been able to exchange poems about love and ladies. "It would be necessary in that case to suppose that this little poem dates from the captivity in Spain of Oton and Florimont"; that is, the years 1372 to 1374.[13] Though there is no conclusive proof for such suppositions, they appear quite probable. We might further imagine that the young poet Granson read Chaucer's *Book of the Duchess* in 1372 before he sailed for Spain (when it is first recorded that he was in England), and then in prison he recalled the cadre of Chaucer's elegy. Braddy lists the following similarities between the *Nouvel an* and the *Duchess*: the scene in set in a wood; the principal characters are a knight and a poet; Granson's knight, like Chaucer's, makes his complaint to himself; and in each work the poet approaches the knight hoping to comfort him.

Other correspondences are found between the English elegy and Granson's *Complainte de Saint Valentin*. This poem has thirty-four eight-line stanzas of the same Monk's Tale form. It is the poet himself who complains here. For the first eleven stanzas he speaks of his inconsolability in the face of the death of his lady. Stating that he cannot love another, nor could he

144

possibly be loved by any who approach her worth, he is resolved to remain alone and dolorous. Then he sees St. Valentine approaching leading the God of Love, who reminds him that he is his sworn subject, and tells him that he must choose a new lady. Furthermore, he need not have any qualms, for Loyalty has agreed to this. The poet responds that he seeks only to lament his mistress and to attain death while engaged in his lamentation. But Amor insists that he at least look at the lady chosen for him; then he can take her or resign himself to his sorrow. The narrator, acknowledging his duty to the god, takes one look and immediately assents to serve the lady humbly all his life. For the last eight stanzas of the work he praises her youth and beauty; she is the most praiseworthy of all the fine ladies in whose company he sees her. He asks that Amor aid him in this affair, for it is now by this lady that he will be cured or receive death. Thus, he concludes, did he follow the command of Amor on St. Valentine's Day.

Braddy notes that the correspondences between the St. Valentine complaint and the *Duchess* supplement those between the *Nouvel an* and Chaucer's work. In the *Saint Valentin* the lover complains about the death of a mistress, and is, like the Black Knight, inconsolable.

The English knight has lost "my worldes welfare" (v. 1040); the French, "tout mon bien en ce monde" (v. 46). The Englishman wishes that death had "taken me" (v. 482); the Frenchman desires "La mort pour mon alegement" (v. 32).[14]

The correspondences are certainly telling, but surely it is easier to imagine that Granson's poems followed Chaucer's. The similarities in diction cited have close parallels in Machaut, as do the narrative analogues. It becomes a question again of who went directly to Machaut, Granson or Chaucer, and all the evidence points to Chaucer, most obviously because of his pervasive use of Machaut throughout the elegy. The Saint Valentine complaint, then, like the New Year's complaint, probably followed the *Duchess*, and seems further to have come after *Songe vert*.

If one accepts the line of succession suggested in this study for the various poems of complaint and comfort, a quite orderly development can be seen. Numerous interrelationships serve to confirm the suggested lineage. For example, the early works of the type have formal complaints in a fixed 16-line stanza and other interspersed lyric set-pieces; on the other hand, the set-pieces are not common in later works, which generally use color of clothing symbolically and are concerned with a loved one who has died. To recapitulate, the order of the works seems to be as follows: Machaut's *Remede de Fortune* (before 1342) is the first of the complaint-and-comfort poems. He imitates this early work in *Fonteinne amoreuse* (1360), but makes the poet, rather than a supernatural being, the chief comforter. Froissart's *Paradys d'Amours* (before 1369) reflects both of Machaut's works, and Chaucer's *Duchess* (1369) in turn uses all three. Froissart's *Espinette amoreuse* (c. 1370) seems to have been written in ignorance of Chaucer's elegy, but again employs the works of Machaut. His *Bleu chevalier* (1372?), however, employs features of the *Duchess* as well as the Machaut poems. *Songe vert* (after 1369), while showing no direct relationship with the later Froissart works, seems almost a sequel of the *Book of the Duchess*. Granson's two complaints (1372-74?) incorporate features from both Chaucer's elegy and *Songe vert*.

Ethel Seaton points out that an English work ascribed to Charles d'Orléans, written around 1437, also has "clear affinities" with *Songe vert*.[15] This work, moreover, which is entitled by its editor *Love's Renewal*, makes use of the *Book of the Duchess*,[16] an indication that the family relationships of *Songe vert* and the *Duchess* were still recognized in mid-fifteenth century. The *Duchess*, of course, had other English progeny, two of the best-known being Lydgate's *Complaint of the Black Knight* and Spenser's *Daphnaïda*.

Consideration of the complaint-and-comfort poems, which has

146

occupied the last three chapters, completes the historical survey of the *dits amoreux* which contributed directly and indirectly to the making of the *Book of the Duchess*. But before concluding, one related vision poem that does not concern love should be taken up, the *Regret Guillaume Comte de Hainault* of Jehan de la Mote.[17] Constance L. Rosenthal has suggested that this work provided Chaucer's model for the vision used as elegy.[18] The historical circumstances of the *Regret* certainly make it probable that Chaucer knew the work, for according to a statement in the poem Jehan wrote it at Queen Philippa's request in 1339, two years after the death of the famous count, who was Philippa's father and the grandfather of John of Gaunt.

In the *Regret* the vision framework provides a setting for the tedious complaints that take up more than 4000 of the 4581 lines. After asking God, Mary, Nature, and the angels for help, the poet relates how one night in a dream it seems that he is wandering about looking for a certain road when he comes into a forest "amoreuse et deduisant." The sweetness of the place bothers rather than pleases him. Then he hears the sound of trumpets, tambourines, and all kinds of musical instruments coming from the direction of a little path that only one man has ever entered:

> Bien vic que c'estoit là endroit,
> Lés une petite sentelette,
> Maubatue et estroitelette,
> C'ains mais en ce siecle mondain,
> Ne au premier ne au darrain,
> N'i avoit c'un seul homme entré;
> Ne sai jou pas en verité
> S'en tamps à venir nus yra.   (ll. 152-159)

He follows the path to a most beautiful castle built on a rock foundation; as he approaches the music he has heard turns to groaning. In answer to his knock and his loud request, "Laisieme ens entrer!" a lady whose clothing is wet from her tears opens a peep-hole and tells him that he might as well go away, for the minstrels have departed and there will never be joy in the castle

147

again. A treacherous robber, she asserts, has stolen thence their "brother, lord, friend, son, and father."

The dreamer responds that nonetheless she should let him in, for perhaps he can write something to comfort them:

> Et s'il plest Dieu, vous en orés
> Cose qui vous confortera,
> Car espoir mes corps en fera
> Aucun dit pour la vostre amour. (ll. 280-283)

The lady cannot allow him to enter, but she leads him to a little window, through which the poet sees many other ladies in all attitudes of lamentation. He asks their names and the name of the prince. She answers that the prince was Guillaume, Count of Hainault, Holland, and Zealand, and also lord of Frisia; she herself is Deboinnaireté, and the others are Humelité, Largece, Hardemens, Proecce, Sens, Loiauté, and so forth, thirty in all. The poet now listens as each of the ladies makes a complaint of a hundred of so lines, each of these followed by a three-stanza *balade*. Deboinnaireté's lament comes first and includes a seventy-line address to death:

> Helas! fausse mors, lasse aymi!
> Fausse mors, qui nul bien n'enorte,
> Hé, fausse mors, que tu m'as morte. (ll. 526-528)

The complaints are filled with similar reproaches of Death and with praise of the count's virtue. After hearing the lamentations, the poet awakens, and he tells the dream to his mistress, the Queen of England, who orders him to make a poem out of it. The poet closes with his name and the date of the work.

Miss Rosenthal notes that the existence of this poem invalidates Professor Kittredge's statement that the *Duchess* is the first poem to use a dream vision for a personal elegy.[19] Besides the fact of the elegy and the historical pertinence of the *Regret* to Chaucer's patrons, she cites as analogous to the *Duchess* certain phrases in the poem of which the description of Blanche may

148

"echo sentiments" (She admits that the description contains no phrase borrowed directly from the *Regret*). She might also have instanced the *petite sentelette* that the poet follows to the castle as possibly having suggested Chaucer's *litel-used wente* (other counterparts of Chaucer's path were noted in Chapter I). And the desire of the poet to comfort the bereaved ladies is similar to the dreamer's expressed purpose in the *Duchess*, though Chaucer's phraseology here undoubtedly derives from *Behaingne*.

The *Regret Guillaume* thus may have suggested some details for the *Duchess* to Chaucer, and it certainly supplied a precedent for an elegy within a dream vision. It should therefore be included among the probable French sources of the *Book of the Duchess*, most of which have been considered in this study. Besides the *Roman de la Rose, Paradys d'Amours, Behaingne, Remede de Fortune*, and *Fonteinne amoreuse*, these include nine other works of Machaut, the *Roman de Troie*, and several other possibilities which are shown in the Appendix. The Appendix provides a rundown of the line-for-line uses by Chaucer of the language of other works, and shows that in addition to the French poems, several Latin works also figure among the originals of Chaucer's poem. Among these are the Bible, Petrus de Riga's *Aurora*, Statius' *Thebaid*, the *Aeneid*, and *Metamorphoses*. The total number of these sources is impressive, as is the extent to which Chaucer uses them while still making the poem his own.

Because of the poet's employment of sources, the *Book of the Duchess* provides a singularly fertile ground for the literary analyst. With most good literature few of the materials which the writer has employed are available to the critic; they are either locked in the author's mind—inaccessible to all, including the writer—or they are lost or unknown, as with the immediate sources for many of the *Canterbury Tales*. But with the *Book of the Duchess* there are known immediate sources for nearly every part, whose relationships to Chaucer's poem may be carefully inspected to determine which elements of the sources and tradition he chose to use, which to discard, and what he added.

149

Analysis of this kind can lead to important understanding of the nature of the resulting poem and to a better comprehension of how Chaucer's imagination—and, by extension, the imagination of other poets—"dissolves, diffuses, dissipates, in order to recreate," and how it "struggles to idealize and unify." One object of this whole investigation of the *dit amoreux* has been to provide such analysis, though there has been little attempt to evaluate the results of it, that being the province of a different kind of study.

EPILOGUE

THE IMPORTANCE OF THE *DITS AMOREUX*

This study has charted the stream of love narratives which found its source in the work of Guillaume de Lorris and flowed into English literature more than a century later primarily by way of the *Book of the Duchess*. The current of the *dit amoreux* continued on throughout Chaucer's works, augmented by and mixed in with other influences, but never lost.

Specific influences on Chaucer are numerous; simple citation of the more important is impressive. The narrative structure of the *Duchess*, ultimately indebted to the French works, recurs in great part in the *Parliament of Fowls* and the *House of Fame*. The love vision machinery of the *dits* is used in the four dream poems, in *Troilus*, and in the Nun's Priest's Tale. The naive comic narrator, related especially to Machaut's persona, is found in all of Chaucer's major poetry, most strikingly perhaps in the *House of Fame* and *Sir Topas*. Important gardens of love in Chaucer's works following the *Duchess* are found in the Prologue to the *Legend* and in the Franklin's and Merchant's Tales. The origins of Chaucer's numerous lovers who resemble the Black Knight, including Troilus and Palemon and Arcite, are certainly French as well as Italian, while the many lover's complaints in Chaucer's poetry which have French ancestry include the laments in *Anelida and Arcite*, *Troilus*, the Knight's Tale, and the Squire's Tale. Elaborate descriptions like that of Blanche are to be found in modified form in *Troilus*, the General Prologue, and the

151

Miller's, Reeve's, and Nun's Priest's Tales. Finally, so great a number of Chaucer's works contain versions of the typical narrative of courtly love as found in the *Duchess* and its French predecessors—or parody or comment on this typical love narrative—that it would be almost to list his works to name them.

Thus Chaucer's works throughout his career are substantially strengthened by specific elements derived from the *dits amoreux*, but these elements represent only a part of the total influence. The French poems also made a more general contribution by providing a counterweight in Chaucer's narratives both to the wit and irony associated with Jean de Meun and to the racy sophistication which is characteristic of Boccaccio. This counterbalancing is less noticeable in later works because the influence of the *dits* is absorbed into that which seems most intrinsically Chaucerian. In *Troilus*, for example, the implicit attitude toward love is certainly less ironic than that of Jean de Meun, and less urbane than that of Boccaccio; and the pace of the narrative is more deliberate than that of the *Filostrato*. At the same time the casual interruption of the story provided by Machaut's main specific contribution to Troilus—Antigone's song—is not disruptive, and the earnest naiveté of its expression is quite consonant with the stance of the narrator and the poet.

In considering such works as the *Book of the Duchess* and the Prologue to the *Legend*, it is important also to understand what aspects are not attributable to the French influence. The books that the narrator reads, the exemplum which precedes and closely parallels the main story of the *Duchess*, the Marian imagery in the description of Blanche,[1] the intercessor Alceste in the Prologue, and elements such as these are features original with Chaucer, a part of that which makes his poems different from and undoubtedly superior to the sources of which he makes such pervasive use.

Of course the works taken up in the study have further interest as influences on fifteenth- and sixteenth-century French

152

poetry, and as works of intrinsic merit. Speculation about influence on later French literature is a matter which lies outside this study; a statement about literary value, on the other hand, is surely relevant. All of the works considered here have some merit. One might notice particularly the intricate allegories of Baudouin de Condé's *Prisons d'Amours* and Jehan Acart's *Prise amoreuse*, which not only are impressive *tours de force* but also provide metaphors effectively expressive of the lovers' trials. The pleasantly dreamlike *Messe des oisiaus* of Jean de Condé, despite its loose structure, successfully combines good poetry with broad humor. Machaut's *Behaingne* marries the debate structure to the conventions of the *dit amoreux* to produce an original and interesting narrative. In the *Dit dou Lyon* the magic island, the lion lover, and particularly the old knight's lecture are inspired creations. The *Fonteinne amoreuse*, as a personal allegory designed to comfort a patron, rivals the *Duchess* in surface appeal. And both the *Paradys d'Amours* and the *Dit dou Bleu Chevalier* of Froissart have genuine lyricism along with well-made stories.

The *Book of the Duchess* itself is of considerable merit, of course; among the poems taken up here it is second in aesthetic value only to Guillaume de Lorris' poem. This study should lead to a larger appreciation of the *Duchess*. To be sure the values of any work do not derive directly from its sources and analogues, but inspection of sources and analogues, when they are important, facilitates analysis. They are particularly important in this poem of Chaucer's, since almost every part has a known immediate source, and every part without exception has a tradition behind it in French literature.

Most of the insights which this study might lead to have been left implicit in it. I have presented the development of the genre and shown the contribution made by the various sources of the *Duchess*; in the Appendix I have detailed Chaucer's indebtedness line by line; but only up to this point have I attempted to make the coverage comprehensive. As I indicated at the beginning, my aim has been primarily to make more accessible and comprehensible material which will be relevant to future criticism of the *Duchess,* Chaucer's work, and the *dits amoreux.*

APPENDIX

SOURCES OF THE DICTION OF THE *BOOK OF THE DUCHESS*

Key

Major Sources:

Beh	Machaut, *Jugement dou Roy de Behaingne*
Fon	Machaut, *Dit de la Fonteinne amoreuse*
RF	Machaut, *Remede de Fortune*
Rose	Guillaume de Lorris (to l. 4058) and Jean de Meun (after l. 4058), *Roman de la Rose*
Par	Froissart, *Paradys d'Amours*

Minor Sources:

Adam	Adam of St. Victor, *Salve Mater Salvatoris*
Aen	Vergil, *Aeneid*
Apoc	*Apocalypse*
Aur	Petrus de Riga, *Aurora*
Boet	Boethius, *Consolation of Philosophy*
Can	*Canticles*
Con	Machaut, *Lay de Confort*
Lyon	Machaut, *Dit dou Lyon*
Met	Ovid, *Metamorphoses*
Nav	Machaut, *Jugement dou Roy de Navarre*
Om	*Ovide moralisé*
Plan	Alanus de Insulis, *De Planctu Naturae*
Regr	Jehan de la Mote, *Regret Guillaume*
Theb	Statius, *Thebaid*
Tour	Watriquet de Condé, *Tournois des dames*
Troi	Benoît de Sainte Maure, *Roman de Troie*
VD	Machaut, *Voir Dit*
Wis	*Wisdom*

1Com	Machaut, *First Complaint*
3Mot	Machaut, *Third Motet*
8Mot	Machaut, *Eighth Motet*
9Mot	Machaut, *Ninth Motet*
38BN	Machaut, *Thirty-Eigth Balade Notée*

Line numbers in parentheses indicate no identified source.
"Cf." indicates less definite or questionable source.

Line Numbers	Major Source	Minor Source
1-8	Par 1-9	
(9-15)		
16-21		Cf. 1Com 7-8
(22)		
23-29		Nav. 109-112
23	Cf. Par 7	
(30-36)		
37	Cf. Beh 125-128	
(38)		
39-43	Cf. RF 1467-69	Cf. Lyon 57-61, 68
42		Cf. Nav 39-42
44-61		Cf. VD 8233-38
45	Par 13	
62-75		Cf. Met XI.410-572
76-105	Cf. Fon 545-557	
106-114	Fon 558-564	
(115-128)		
129-139	Cf. Fon 571-579	
(140-143)		
144-148		Om XI.3427-30; Cf. Met XI.585-588
152		Met XI.586
153-154		Met XI.585-587
145-156	Fon 590-592	
157-159		Theb X.86, 97-99
160-162		Om XI.3450-55; Cf. Met XI.600-604
163-165		Theb X.86-87, 95-97
166		Met X.612
167-168	Par 28; Fon 651-652	
169	Fon 649	

Line Numbers	Major Source	Minor Source
170-171		Theb X. 84
(172-173)		
174-177		Theb X.112-115
178-183		Cf. Theb XI.132-133
184-185	Fon 631-632	
(186-190)		
191	Fon 619-620	
192-200	Cf. Fon 658-662	Cf. Met XI.653-657
201-205		Aen II.776-779, 784
206-207		Met XI.669-670
(208)		
209-211		Cf. Aen II.789
(212-217)		
218-220	Fon 699-700	
221-223	Cf. Par 19-22	
(224-241)		
242-245	Par 14-18	
246-269	Fon 807-810; Cf. Par 18-21	
(270-271)		
272-275	Par 14,31	
(276-283)		
284-287	Rose 7-10	
(288-290)		
291-292	Rose 45-47,88	
293-296	Rose 75	
(297-300)		
301-302	Rose 661-662	
(303)		
304-305	Rose 484-485, 705	
306-309	Rose 667-670	
309-311	Rose 487-492, 1619-22	
312-316	Cf. Rose 706-708, 663-674	
317-320	Rose 73-75, 101	
321-334		Cf. Tour 123-128
331-332	Rose 20831-32	
335-338	Cf. Beh 15-19	
339-343	Beh 13-14; Cf. Rose 124-125	
344-386	Cf. Paradys 903-953	
368	Cf. Beh 421	

157

Line Numbers	Major Source	Minor Source
(387)		
388-397	Beh 25-27, 1204-11	Lyon 325-331, 499-509
398-401	Cf. Beh 28-31	Cf. Regr 152-159
402-403	Rose 8411-18	
405-409	Rose 8427-30	
410-415	Rose 55-62	
416-435	Rose 1361-82	
436-442	Rose 12790-96	
(443-445)		
446-447	Cf. Rose 1428-31, 1471	
(448-451)		
452-454	Cf. Beh 50, 57-59	
(455-474)		
475-486	Beh 193-201	Cf. 3Mot 1-8
487-499	Cf. Beh 206-215	
(500-501)		
502-513	Cf. Beh 56-69	
(514-516)		
517-518	Cf. Beh 59-60	
519-525	Beh 70-74	
526-528	Beh 75-78	
(529-531)		
532-533	Beh 85-86	
(534-535)		
536-538	Cf. Beh 86	
(539-549)		
546-554	Beh 87-92	
555	Cf. Beh 78-80	
(556-557)		
558-566	Cf. Beh 93-101	
(567-582)		
583-586	Cf. Beh 195-198	Apoc ix.6
(587-588)		
589		Cf. Met X.43-44
(590-598)		
599-615	Cf. Beh 177-187	
599-600		Plan I.1-2
600	RF 1198	
(616-617)		
618-619	Cf. Rose 6557-60	

Line Numbers	Major Source	Minor Source
620-621	RF 1054-56	
622	RF 1167-68	
623-625		Cf. Boet II Pr. I
626		8Mot 9
(627)		
628-629	Cf. Rose 8908-13	8Mot 7-8
(630-631)		
632		8Mot 6
633-634	RF 1162	
635	RF 918	
636-641	Cf. Rose 6744-46	9Mot 44-47
642	RF 1138	
(643)		
644	Cf. Rose 6624	
645-646	Beh 1072-74	
647	RF 1052-53	
648-649	Beh 1078-80	
(650-652)		
653-654	Rose 6711-12	
(655-658)		
659-661	Rose 6652-55	Cf. RF 1190-91
662-664	Rose 6691-92	
(665-672)		
673-674	RF 1113-14	
(675-692)		
693-696		Con 10-13
(697-708)		
709		Cf. Met X. 40-41
(710-716)		
717-719	Rose 5844-50	
(720-725)		
726-734	Cf. Rose 13174-259	
731-734		Cf. Nav 2095-2118
735-737	Cf. Rose 1439-48	Cf. 7Mot 38,42-44
738-739	Cf. Rose 9203-06	
(740-748)		
749-752	Beh 253-256	
(753-758)		
759-763	Beh 261-264	
764-770	Beh 123-133	

159

Line Numbers	Major Source	Minor Source
771-776	Beh 265-273	
777-778	RF 61-63	
779-784	RF 26-30	
785-792	RF 35-40	
793-796	RF 23-25	
797-804	RF 45-51	
805-815	Beh 281-285	
812-813		8Mot 16-20
(816)		
817-829	Beh 286-290	
820-829		Adam
(830-832)		
833-834	RF 197-199	
835-836	RF 71-72	
837-843	RF 95-99, 102-103	
844-845		Cf. Con 164-166
(846-847)		
848-858	Beh 297-303	
859-874	Beh 312, 316, 318, 321-330	
(875-882)		
883-887	Beh 331-335	
(884-894)		
895-903	Beh 292-296	
904-905	Beh 356-358	
905		Cf. Cant v.10
906	RF 1629-30	
907-911	Beh 397-403	
912-913	Beh 411-414	
(914-917)		
918	Beh 580-581	
919-926	RF 217-224	
927-932	RF 225-230, 234	
933-936	RF 234-236	
937	RF 238	
(938)		
939-947	Beh 361-363	
946		Cant vii.4
948-951	RF 54-56	
952-957	Beh 364-377	
958-960	Beh 380-383	

Line Numbers	Major Source	Minor Source
961-985		Cf. Wis vii.26
963-965	Cf. Rose 7410-13	
966-974	RF 167-174	
972		Cf. Cant v.10
981-984	Cf. Rose 15977-98	
985-987	Cf. RF 123-124	
(988-1023)		
1024-32		Cf. Lyon 1368-70, 1420-57
(1033-34)		
1035-41	Beh 148-153, 156-161	
(1042-55)		
1056-66	Cf. RF 107-134, Beh 421-425	Cf. 38BN 1-23
1067-71		Cf. Troi 21838-22334
(1072-79)		
1080-85	Rose 8605-12	
(1086-87)		
1088-94	RF 89-94	
1095-1100	RF 135-144	
1101	RF 64-65	
1102-07	RF 295-302	
1108-11	Cf. RF 131-134	Cf. Lyon 207-212
(1112-15)		
1116-25	Cf. Beh 1140-47	
(1126-45)		
1146-51	RF 357-364	
1152-54	Rose 1996-97	
1155-57	RF 401-403	
(1158-61)		
1162-69		Aur
(1170)		
1171-74	Cf. RF 401-403, 430	
1175-80	Cf. RF 431-463	
(1181-82)		
1183-91	Cf. Beh 453-456	
1192	Cf. Beh 466	
(1193-94)		
1195-98	Beh 461-462; Cf. RF 1671-83	
(1199-1202)		
1203-18	Cf. Beh 467-476	

Line Numbers	Major Source	Minor Source
1216	Cf. RF 696	
1219	Cf. Beh 505	
(1220-25)		
1226-30	Cf. Beh 656-658	
(1231-35)		
1236-38	Cf. Beh 509-512	
1239-44	Cf. Beh 541-548	
(1245)		
1246-49		Cf. Troi 26113-94
1250-51	RF 751-752	
(1252-57)		
1258-67	Beh 592-598	
(1268-69)		
1270	Beh 641, 670	
1271	Cf. Beh 610	
(1272)		
1273	Cf. RF 4074-75	
(1274)		
1275-78	Beh 622-625	
(1279-84)		
1285-86	RF 139-140	
(1287-88)		
1289-97	Beh 166-176	
(1298-1323)		
1324-25	Par 1685-92	
(1326-29)		
1330	Par 1693-95	
(1331-33)		
1334	Par 1722-23	

162

NOTES

NOTES FOR INTRODUCTION

[1] *Chaucer and the French Tradition* (Berkeley, 1957), p. 1.
[2] Harvard Studies and Notes in Philology and Literature, VI (Boston, 1899).
[3] Chaucer Society, 2nd Series, XXXIX (London, 1907).
[4] "Chaucer and Froissart," *Englische Studien*, XXVI (1899), 321-336; "Chauceriana," *MP*, VII (1910), 465-483; and "Guillaume de Machaut and *The Book of the Duchess*," *PMLA*, XXX (1915), 1-24.

NOTES FOR CHAPTER I

[1] This is a common distinction, most recently set forth by Charles Muscatine in *Chaucer and the French Tradition* (Berkeley, 1957), pp. 11-97. Alan M. F. Gunn, in *The Mirror of Love* (Lubbock, 1952), pp. 415-523, questions with some cogency the classification of Jean as "bourgeois."

Gunn also takes issue with the idea (expressed here) that the *Rose* is two poems. A premise of his book is that the *Rose* is a unified work rather than, as in the interpretation of C. S. Lewis, two separate entities yoked together only by Jean de Meun's audacity. Gunn says that, whereas Lewis claims that Jean is uninterested in Guillaume's subject, a more accurate statement is that Jean is not interested in Guillaume's narrative, for Jean's continuation consists of an extension and an expansion of Guillaume's treatment of the subject of love. But even Gunn's viewpoint acknowledges that Guillaume and Jean achieve very different results: Guillaume a courtly Art of Love, and Jean a comprehensive discussion of the whole subject of love. For a fuller discussion see Lewis' *Allegory of Love* (New York, 1958), pp. 137-142;

Gunn, pp. 141-198; and Lewis' review of Gunn, *MÆ*, XXII (1953), 27-31.

² The subsequent analysis of the *Roman de la Rose* is based on the edition of Ernest Langlois, Société des anciens textes français, 5 vols. (Paris, 1914-24). Citations of this work herein are to this edition.

³ This is C. S. Lewis' insight. His gloss of the whole allegory is most enlightening, if not flawless. See *Allegory of Love*, pp. 114-136.

⁴ He has promised to tell in the remainder of the work

> coment li murs fu levez
> E li chastiauz riches e forz
> Qu'Amors prist puis par ses esforz. (ll. 3502-04)

⁵ *A Preface to Chaucer* (Princeton, 1963), pp, 463-464. Professor Robertson's theory that the Black Knight is an alter ego of the poet suggests a possible allegorical dimension to the work, but I am convinced that the Knight literally should be seen as John of Gaunt. Robertson espouses his position at length in his essay, "The Historical Setting of Chaucer's *Book of the Duchess*," in *Mediaeval Studies in Honor of Urban Tigner Holmes, Jr.* (Chapel Hill, 1965), pp. 169-195.

⁶ Ll. 1318-19. References to Chaucer's works herein are to the edition of F. N. Robinson, *The Works of Geoffrey Chaucer*, 2nd ed. (New York, 1957).

⁷ Ll. 40-41, 45-54. References to Machaut's works herein, except where noted, are to the edition of Ernest Hoepffner, *Les Œuvres de Guillaume de Machaut*, 3 vols. (Paris, 1908-21). For Hoepffner's analysis of the anagram see III, xxvi-xxvii. In a later chapter it will be seen that *Fonteinne amoreuse* provides also a precedent for the poem which involves a poet's ducal patron and his wife.

⁸ Chaucer even follows Guillaume in his mistaken attribution of Cicero's work to Macrobius, who of course wrote a commentary on the classical work.

⁹ Ll. 20-40. Birds were a familiar prop for that which is loosely designated *chanson d'aventure*. The beginning of *Behaingne* fits in very nicely with the description given in Wells' *Manual* for this genre: "The Poet tells that he went out a-pleasuring in a wood or the fields, or went to church, where he met a fair maid or a distressed lady, or a penitent man, or heard monks or a bird singing—and then relates what he learned from the person encountered." John E. Wells, *A Manual of the Writings in Middle English* (New Haven, 1926), p. 489. The beginning of the dream in the *Duchess* obviously owes something to this kind of opening—but by way of the *Rose*.

¹⁰ Ll. 42-61. References to Froissart's works herein are to Auguste Scheler, ed., *Œuvres de Froissart: Poésies*. 3 vols. (Brussels, 1870-72).

¹¹ Ll. 46-51. References to Watriquet's works are to Auguste Scheler, ed. *Dits de Watriquet de Couvin* (Brussels, 1868).

¹² References to these poems are to Henry A. Todd, ed., *Le Dit de la Panthère d'Amours*, SATF (Paris, 1883); and to Friedrich Stehlich, ed., *Li Romanz de la Poire* (Halle, 1881).

¹³ References to Jean's works and to his father's are to Auguste Scheler, ed., *Dits et contes de Baudouin de Condé et de son fils Jean de Condé*, 3 vols. (Brussels, 1866-67).

¹⁴ These correspondences are as follows (lines of the *Duchess* precede the colons and the equivalent lines of the *Rose* follow them): 402-409: 8411-18, 8427-30; 410-415:55-62; 416-442:1361-82 and 12790 (for *Argus*).

¹⁵ For the tradition behind Guillaume de Lorris' garden see the chapter, "The Ideal Landscape," in Ernst Curtius, *European Literature and the Latin Middle Ages*, tr. Willard R. Trask (New York, 1953), pp. 183-202; also D. W. Robertson, Jr., "The Doctrine of Charity in Medieval Gardens," *Speculum*, XXVI (1951), 24-49. A number of medieval gardens are cited in Oliver M. Johnston, "The description of the emir's orchard in Floire et Blancheflor," *Zeitschrift für Romanische Philologie*, XXXII (1908), 705-710. In a note to the *Roman de la Rose* (l. 78), Langlois remarks that "Le prototype de tous ces vergers parait être le paradis d'Amours de Tibulle."

¹⁶ In this *balade* Froissart mentions the rose, violet, lily, bluet, columbine, peony, lily-of-the-valley and the heliotrope. In domestic flowers this list surpasses Guillaume de Lorris', whose plentiful enumeration of vegetation is mainly taken up with fruit trees and exotic spice plants.

¹⁷ *Lyon*: "Dragons, serpens, escorpions,/De toutes generations,/Buglos, chameus, tygres, pantheres,/etc." (ll. 381-406.) *Panthère*: Beasts of all colors, "Lyons, liepars, et autres bestes,/Faisans par le bois grans tempestes;/De sanglés et de pors sauvages/Retentissoit tous li boscages;/Ours y avoit et unicornes,/Et autres bestes qui ont cornes,/Cerfs, dains, chevriaus, sauvages bous,/Qui d'arbrissiaus broustent les brous,/Aveques les sauvages chievres;/E s'i avoit connins et lievres,/Leus et gourpis et heriçons,/Que ont poignans les peliçons;/Et autres que nommer ne sai" (ll. 67-79).

¹⁸ Oliver F. Emerson, in an informative article in which he glosses the hunting terms which Chaucer employs, attempts to prove that a station beside a tree was too menial a job for one of Chaucer's rank at

court, but his substitute explanation is not convincing. "Chaucer and Medieval Hunting," *Romanic Review*, XIII (1922), 132-133.

[19] References to the *Chasse aux médisants* are to the edition of A. Mercier in *Annales du Midi*, VI (1894), 465-494.

[20] Chaucer also draws on Ovid, Statius, Froissart, and perhaps Vergil for this exemplum. For a full analysis see my article on the sources of Chaucer's Seys and Alcyone to appear in *Medium Ævum*.

[21] John M. Manly, "Chaucer and the Rhetoricians," *Proceedings of the British Academy*, XII (1926), 100.

[22] Former puzzlement and disapproval concerning Chaucer's introduction have in the main given way to modern solutions and approval. Noteworthy discussions, illuminating the parallel between the early portions of the *Duchess* and the elegy, are found in Wolfgang Clemen, *Der Junge Chaucer* (Bochum-Langendreer, 1938), pp. 29-71; Bertrand Bronson, "*The Book of the Duchess* Reopened," *PMLA*, LXVII (1952), 863-881, and *In Search of Chaucer* (Toronto, 1960), pp. 34-43; Donald C. Baker, "Imagery and Structure in Chaucer's *Book of the Duchess*," *Studia Neophilologica*, XXX (1958), 17-26; and Robert M. Lumiansky, "The Bereaved Narrator in Chaucer's *The Book of the Duchess*," *Tulane Studies in English*, IX (1959), pp. 5-17.

[23] The Black Knight's lyric (ll. 475-486), in which he speaks of the death of his beloved, is, after all, a *lay* composed by a knight-poet which may or may not be a report of fact.

[24] D. W. Robertson has some relevant comments about the prologue of *Navarre* in his *Preface to Chaucer*, pp. 234-236.

NOTES FOR CHAPTER II

[1] Baudouin de Condé, the father of Jean, was court *trouvère* to Margaret of Flanders; his editor surmises that his poetic activity fell between 1240 and 1280. Auguste Scheler, ed., *Dits et contes de Baudouin de Condé et de son fils Jean de Condé* (Brussels, 1866-67), I, xiii. The first date seems early, since Jean was still writing in 1337, ninety-seven years later.

Though *Prisons d'Amours* differs in subject matter from Baudouin's general work and does not appear with the body of his poetry in several manuscripts, Scheler considers its ascription to him soundly based. Despite the fact that Baudouin was "si humble, si chaste et si honnête," says the editor, *Prisons d'Amours* "rappelle bien pour quelques points qui s'y trouvent traités, l'auteur du dit de la Rose [one of Baudouin's other works], et, quant au côté moral, celui qui se place au point de vue du XIIIe siècle n'admettra guère l'incompatibilité entre le poëte qui prêche l'honneur et la vertu et le troubadour soupirant après les faveurs d'une châtelaine mariée" (I, 505).

2 *Origins and Sources of the Court of Love*, Harvard Studies and Notes in Philology and Literature, VI (Boston, 1899), p. 66.

3 Neilson's study of the Middle English *Court of Love* reviews the tradition of this kind of allegory quite fully.

4 References to *Salu d'Amours* are to the complete edition of Philippe's poems, edited by Hermann Suchier, *Œuvres Poétiques de Philippe de Remi, Sire de Beaumanoir*, SATF, 2 vols. (Paris, 1884-85). Two romances, *La Manekine* (a version of the legend from which the *Man of Law's Tale* is derived) and *Jehan et Blonde*, comprising over 14,000 lines, make up the greater part of Philippe's poetical work. Also among his poems is the 520-line *Conte d'Amours*, which would be of interest in this study if the narrator's dream vision in the middle of the poem were not missing from the manuscript; what is left is chiefly conversation between the narrator and his reluctant beloved.

A thorough biographical study of this poet-jurist was made by Henri-Léonard Bordier, *Philippe de Remi, sire de Beaumanoir, juris-consulte et poète nationale de Beauvaisis*, 2 vols. (Paris, 1869-73). Of Philippe's legal writings Suchier comments, "L'éloge de Beaumanoir comme jurisconsulte n'est plus à faire: il est généralement reconnu que dans ses *Coutumes* où il promet seulement d'enseigner *le droit uzé et accoustumé en le conté de Clermont* il a su établir les fondements généraux du droit coutumier français, exposer ses idées avec une supériorité d'esprit et une étendue de vues peu communes de son temps, et discuter les plus difficiles questions avec une clarté et une concision dont la langue française n'avait pas encore fait preuve" (I, i).

5 *Origins and Sources*, p. 120.

6 Ed. Marcelle Thiébaux, *SP*, LXII (1965), 531-545. The unduplicated lines appearing in the work's two extant manuscripts total 337.

7 A somewhat harsh notice on the *Cerf amoreus* in the *Histoire littéraire de la France* (*HLF*) describes it as "not truly a poem about the hunt, but a parallel in 320 obscure and awkward lines, which makes the lover the hunter and the lady the *cerf d'amour*." V[ictor] L[e] C[lerc], XXIII, 290.

8 *La Prise amoreuse: allegorische Dichtung aus dem XIV. Jahrhundert* (Dresden, 1910), ed. Ernest Hoepffner. For more information about this poem see Antoine Thomas' notice on "Frère Jean Acart" in *HLF*,

XXXVII, 412-418, and the dissertation of Paul Weingärtner, *Quellenverhältnis und Allegorie in der Prise amoreuse des Jehan Acart de Hesdin* (Würzberg, 1926).

9 Less egregious inconsistencies than those in *Prise amoreuse* evoked from C. S. Lewis criticism of the allegory in *Roman de la Rose*; he found Jalosie, Ami and the Duenna troublesome because they are real people mixed in with personifications (*Allegory of Love*, pp. 118-119). But no poet of the *dits amoreux* seems to have been overly scrupulous about the logical integrity of his allegorical representations.

10 Hoepffner's edition numbers only 1914 lines. When he edited the poem he used the single manuscript then identified; today four manuscripts and the leaf of a fifth are known (and testify to a modest popularity for the poem in its day). See Hoepffner's supplementary article, "Zur 'Prise amoreuse' von Jehan Acart de Hesdin," *Zeitschrift für romanische Philologie*, XXXVIII (1917), 513-527.

11 Ed. A. Mercier, *Annales du Midi*, VI (1894), 465-494. Mercier says that this poem is the oldest extant literary work in French by a man of the land of *langue d'oc*. The poem is 751 lines long and dates from 1338.

12 For a brief treatment of these German hunts see Neilson, pp. 120-123.

13 Chaucer's only other important description of the hunt is found in his brief relation of Theseus' and Ypolita's hunt of the hart in the *Knight's Tale*, A. 1673-95.

14 "Chaucer and Medieval Hunting," *RR*, XIII (1922), 115-150.

15 Ll. 1310-15. When the Black Knight is referred to as "this kyng," it becomes probable that he is Octavian himself, whom the dreamer has been told is "here faste by" at the time he joined the hunt. This identification applied to John of Gaunt is not unnatural. Certainly if one were to construct a Carolingian romance typology for England at this time, Octavian would be a legitimate representative of John. Edward III's surrogate obviously could then be Charlemagne, and the Black Prince's Roland. It would be complimentary to John and inoffensive to others to present him in the guise of the legendary courtly Emperor of Rome.

16 *Hert* was potentially ambiguous in Middle English as it is in Modern English, as has been recognized by other interpreters of this passage. Donald C. Baker says, "I seriously suggest a pun on 'hert' for 'herte,' meaning heart, or soul-searching." "Imagery and Structure in Chaucer's *Book of the Duchess*," *Studia Neophilologica*, XXX (1958), 23. One might equally argue that *hert* as *herte* signifies *beloved*.

17 Thiébaux, p. 531.

1 Ed Friedrich Stehlich (Halle, 1881).
2 Thibaut's poem is the first of the *dits amoreux* to employ this device according to Urban T. Holmes, *History of Old French Literature*, 2nd ed. (New York, 1962), p. 305. Machaut especially was fond of hiding character identifications in anagrams.
3 For suplementary discussions of *Poire*, see Stehlich's introduction, pp. 1-31; É[mile] L[ittré], "Poèmes d'aventure: La Poire," *HLF*, XXII, 870-879; and Neilson, *Origins and Sources of the Court of Love*, pp. 56-59.
4 Jean is not always anxious to cite his medieval sources by name. Ernest Langlois remarks, "L'empressement excessif de Jean de Meun à citer les noms des auteurs anciens toutes les fois que directement ou indirectement il leur fait le moindre emprunt, contraste avec le soin qu'il prend de dissimuler des dettes bien plus importantes contractées envers des auteurs modernes." *Origines et sources du Roman de la Rose* (Paris, 1891), p. 173.
5 Ed. I. C. Lecompte, *MP*, VIII (1910), 63-86. The standard dating of the poem is 1250-1300. The work consists of 142 decasyllabic quatrains, each quatrain having a single rhyme. Most of the poems considered in this study are, of course, in octosyllabic couplets.
6 "Donne me a boire" (Strophe 37, line d).
7 Lecompte, p. 69.
8 The poet obviously confounds the *phoenix* with the *sphinx*.
9 Wendelin Foerster charts the correspondences between the two poems in his edition of *De Venus la deese d'amor: altfranzösische Minnegedicht aus dem XIII. Jahrhundert* (Bonn, 1880), p. 45. References to *De Venus* herein are to this edition.
    Borrowings made in *De Venus* from *Dou vrai chiment d'Amours* are noted by A. Långfors in his edition of that work, *Romania*, XLV (1918-19), 205-19. *Dou Vrai Chiment*, no narrative but rather a three-hundred-line "traité sur l'amour sincère et l'amour déloyal," provides the source for twenty-three additional quatrains of *De Venus*. Långfors lists the parallels on p. 207.
10 The matter of the dream frame will be taken up in detail in Chapter VII below, when Froissart's *Paradys d'Amours*, which provided the source for the dream frame of the *Duchess*, is discussed.
11 Ed. Henry A. Todd, SATF (Paris, 1883).
12 This same motif is found in Machaut's *Fonteinne amoreuse*, where the lover prays that Morpheus will let the lady know his love as he let Alcyone know the death of Seys. Chaucer in the *Duchess* transmutes the prayer for a vision in Machaut's poem into a request for sleep.

[13] "Chaucer and the Panthère d'Amours," in *Britannica Festschrift für Hermann M. Flasdieck*, ed. Wolfgang Iser and Hans Schabram (Heidelberg, 1960), pp. 51-61.

[14] Wilbur O. Sypherd, *Studies in Chaucer's House of Fame*, Chaucer Society, 2nd series, XXXIX (London, 1909).

[15] *De Venus* is an exception in this respect among the early episodic *dits*, since it is told in the third person, the narrator not being a participant in the action.

[16] *Les trois chanoinesses de Cologne*, ll. 80-84. Citations of Watriquet's work are to Auguste Scheler, ed., *Dits de Watriquet de Couvin* (Brussels, 1868). The scanty information about the poet and his work which is available has been printed in Scheler's introduction and notes to the poems, and in C[harles-Victor] L[anglois], "Watriquet, ménèstral et poète français," *HLF*, XXXV, 394-421.

[17] D'autre mestier ne sai user
   Que de conter biaus dis et faire;
   Je ne me mesle d'autre affaire.
   Watriquet m'apelent aucun
   De Couving, et presque chascun,
   Et sui sires de Verjoli
                     (*Tournois des dames*, ll. 436-441)

[18] Four (mostly) complete, one partial are extant. In addition, a number of his poems are included in various manuscript anthologies.

[19] Auguste Scheler, *Dits et contes de Baudouin de Condé et de son fils Jean de Condé*, 3 vols. (Brussels, 1866-67).

[20] "Jean de Condé, ménèstral et poète français," *HLF*, XXXV, 421-422.

[21] These manuscripts are discussed in Scheler's preface to Jean's poetry, III, xi-xv.

[22] This is a didactic allegory similar to the *Tournois des dames*.

NOTES FOR CHAPTER IV

[1] Hoepffner, I, xii. Much of the information used in this biographical resumé is derived from Hoepffner's introduction, I, xi-xliii. V.-F. Chichmaref's introduction to his edition of Machaut's *Poésies lyriques*, 2 vols. (Paris, 1909) furnishes additional biographical data.

[2] *Œuvres complètes de Eustache Deschamps*, ed. le marquis de Queux de Saint-Hilaire and Gaston Raynaud, SATF (Paris, 1878-1904), I, 243-246.

[3] III, 259-260.

4 Hoepffner, I, i. Machaut's lyrics are collected in Chichmaref's edition. Hoepffner's edition of the *Œuvres* is made up mostly of Machaut's first eight long narratives. His other works are published in various places: Paulin Paris, ed., *Le Livre du Voir Dit de Guillaume de Machaut* (Paris, 1875); L. de Mas-Latrie, ed., *La Prise d'Alexandrie ou Chronique du roi Pierre Ier de Lusignan* (Geneva, 1877); Karl Young, ed. "The Dit de la Harpe of Guillaume de Machaut," *in Essays in Honor of A. Feuillerat*, ed. Henri M. Peyre (New Haven, 1943). Machaut's *Dit de la Marguerite* is printed only in Prosper Tarbé's old collection of the *Œuvres de Guillaume de Machaut* (Paris, 1849), pp. 123-129. There are also published collections of Machaut's musical works.

5 *Histoire des Lettres* (*Histoire de la nation française*, Gabriel Hanotaux, ed., XII [Paris, 1921]), p. 465.

6 Other works of Chaucer also evidence use of Machaut's lyrics. Antigone's song in *Troilus* (ll. 827-875) is substantially indebted to Machaut's *Paradis d'Amour*. And Madeline Fabin, in her article "On Chaucer's Anelida and Arcite," *MLN*, XXXIV (1919), 266-272, concludes that Chaucer in the *Anelida* used Machaut's *Lai de Plour* and the *Lai de la Souscie*.

7 See the chart of eleven manuscript collections of Machaut's poetry provided by Chichmaref, *Poésies lyriques*, I, lxxvi-lxxvii.

8 4814 lines. *Voir Dit* and *Prise d'Alexandrie* are longer. Hoepffner dates the *Alerion* between 1342 and 1357, probably before 1349.

9 Pp. xxxii-xxxiii. For a brief appreciation of *Voir Dit*, see Gustave Cohen, "Le *Voir Dit* de Guillaume de Machaut," *Les Lettres Romanes*, I (1947), 99-111.

10 Machaut's narrator, who is particularly interesting for his relationship to Chaucer's *persona*, will be discussed in the next chapter.

11 Gardiner Stillwell, "Analogues to Chaucer's Manciple's Tale in the Ovide moralisé and Machaut's Voir-Dit," *PQ*, XIX (1940), 133-138.

12 Wilbur O. Sypherd, *Studies in Chaucer's House of Fame* (London, 1907), p. 10.

13 "Chaucer Mentions a Book," *MLN*, LVII (1942), 28-31.

14 "A New Interpretation of the *Parlement of Foules*," *MP*, XVIII (1920), 4.

15 Chichmaref's table of manuscript contents (*Poésies lyriques*, I, lxxvi-lxxvii) shows the *Alerion* in seven of twelve manuscripts, always surrounded by narratives which Chaucer employed.

16 See Emerson's "Chaucer's First Military Service," *RR*, III (1912), 354-355.

¹⁷ See John L. Lowes, "The Prologue of the *Legend of Good Women* as Related to the French *Marguerite* Poems and to the *Filostrato*," *PMLA*, XIX (1904), 593-683. The *Dit de la Marguerite* is not found in many of the manuscript collections of Machaut's works (3 of 12 listed by Chichmaref) and may have circulated separately for the most part.

Though Chaucer's account of the fall of Pierre de Lusignan takes only a stanza in the Monk's Tale ("De Petro Rege de Cipro," B. 3581-88), Haldeen Braddy presents rather convincing evidence that Machaut's *Prise d'Alexandrie* provided the basis for it. "The Two Petros in the 'Monkes Tale,'" *PMLA*, L (1935), 78-80.

¹ See Neilson, *Origins and Sources of the Court of Love*, pp. 31-40, for a summary and discussion of many of these poems. The standard treatment of the medieval Latin debate poems is Hans Walther, *Das Streitgedicht in der lateinischen Litteratur des Mittelalters* (Munich, 1920).

² Ed. Alfons Hilka and Otto Schumann, *Carmina Burana*, 3 vols. (Heidelberg, 1930-41), II, 94-103.

³ *Behaingne* seems to have been the most commonly known of all of Machaut's work. See Hoepffner, I, lxiv.

⁴ George L. Kittredge, "Chauceriana," *MP*, VII (1910), 465-483; and "Guillaume de Machaut and the *Book of the Duchess*," *PMLA*, XXX (1915), 1-24.

⁵ For the aspects of the elegy in question, no further influence need be taken into account. Granson's works and the *Songe Vert*, which have been alleged as models, probably post-date Chaucer's work. See Chapter VIII below.

⁶ Ll. 743-744; repeated in almost the exact words in ll. 1137-38, and 1305-06.

⁷ For ll. 23-29 of the *Duchess* Chaucer used ll. 109-112 from the Prologue of *Navarre*.

⁸ Robert M. Estrich has discussed this parallel quite thoroughly in "Chaucer's Prologue to the *Legend of Good Women* and Machaut's *Le Jugement dou Roy de Navarre*," *SP*, XXVI (1939), 20-39. Estrich does not deny the other influences pointed out by Lowes in his article on the Prologue, *PMLA*, XIX (1904), 593-683; he simply asserts the primacy of *Navarre's* influence on the general plan.

⁹ Of the five stories from classical legend which the ladies narrate, four (Dido, Ariadne, Medea, and Thisbe) have counterparts in Chaucer's

legends, and the fifth (Hero) is among the stories envisioned in Chaucer's plan.

10 *Geoffrey Chaucer and the Development of His Genius* (Boston, 1934), p. 120. The only "essay at humour" which Lowes cites here is "that delicious bit in *La Fonteinne Amoreuse* when Iris for a second time attempts to waken Morpheus, who has meantime gone to sleep again, and when the kindly but somnolent deity opens *un petiot*—just a tiny bit—*one* eye." Chaucer uses this touch in his *exemplum* in the *Duchess*, ll. 184-185.

11 The symbolism of the rabbit as the object of the love hunt has been often mentioned, and is well documented by D. W. Robertson in *Preface to Chaucer* (Princeton, 1963), esp. p. 113 and figs. 25-26. As Robertson says, the ambiguity in French poetry is reinforced by the similarity of *con* and *conin*. Machaut, however, uses the unequivocal *lievre*.

12 It may be that Froissart had a concept of poetic mirth which did not allow for the broadly humorous or whimsical touches. Though in *Paradys d'Amours* he was obviously following Machaut in having the narrator pray to Morpheus, he did not repeat the proposed thank-offering of a featherbed and night-cap found in his source (*Fonteinne amoreuse*, ll. 808-810), a comic touch which Chaucer went back from Froissart to Machaut to pick up and elaborate upon. This is likewise true of Machaut's humorous depiction of Morpheus, which Froissart had every opportunity to use, but chose not to; Chaucer, of course, again capitalized on the comedy that Machaut suggested to him here. Froissart's introduction to *L'Espinette* is both charming and amusing, but restrained.

NOTES TO CHAPTER VI

1 Machaut uses the rhyme scheme aaabaaabbbbabbba for Complaint #6 (Chichmaref, I) and for the complaints which are found in *Remede de Fortune* and *Fonteinne amoreuse*; and Froissart uses the form for similar complaints in *Paradys d'Amours* and *L'Espinette amoreuse*. Chaucer uses it in *Anelida and Arcite*, ll. 256-271, 317-332. The line lengths of the Frenchmen differ from Chaucer's, however. Machaut and Froissart use an eight or ten-syllable line, broken every fourth line with four syllables; Chaucer uses octosyllabic lines broken every fourth line with ten syllables.

2 *Poire*, discussed in Chapter III above, is commonly accepted as

preceding Jean's part of the *Rose*, but the similarity of the appearances of Raison in the two poems may indicate the precedence of Jean's work. Elsewhere Thibaut has obviously borrowed freely from Guillaume de Lorris' part.

3 II, iii-iv.

4 II, xxxv.

5 For a full discussion of the Boethian elements, see Hoepffner, II, xvii-xxxiv.

6 Esperence describes this shield (ll. 1863-1934) as having a red heart on a blue field; the heart is stuck through with ə black arrow that has a burning silver point. An indication that the depiction of the shield was considered an especially notable ornament of the poem is the fact that the whole work is entitled *L'Escu Bleu* in one manuscript.

7 Supporting his idea that there is a *tableau* of lyric pieces in *Remede de Fortune*, in which a single specimen of each current type is presented, Hoepffner says that the *balade* previously sung by Esperence is properly called a *baladele*, and should be differentiated from the *balade* sung here. See II, xliv-xlvii.

8 The Boethian aspect of the Dreamer's relationship to the Black Knight is probably accountable to the influence of the *Roman de la Rose* and the *Consolation* itself as well as *Remede de Fortune*. I take this up in a separate paper, "Several Versions of the Boethian Situation in Chaucer."

9 Lay #8 (Chichmaref, II). He states in this lay that some are never satisfied with the gifts of Amour, however great; others never aspire to more than a sweet look from the lady, or simply permission to love her loyally. He goes on to claim that when the lover gets what he desires, however modest his desire, then he has *merci*:

> Car avis m'est que mercy autre chose
> N'est fors avoir ce qu'amans plus desire,
> Et s'il ha son desir sans contredire,
> Il a merci dont en pais se repose.   (ll. 33-36)

On the other hand, the lover who is never satisfied never has mercy, for mercy is sufficiency:

> Si vueil merci souffissance apeler
> Et ensement souffissance mercy.   (ll. 41-42)

10 III, xxxi.

11 In footnote 1 of my article on "The Sources of Chaucer's Seys and Alcyone" (to appear in *Medium Aevum*), I point out the indebtedness of *Duchess* 106-114 to *Fonteinne* 558-564 and *Duchess* 218-220 to

Fonteinne 699-700. The relationship of *Duchess* 155-156 and 242-269 to *Fonteinne* 591-594 and 807-810 is documented in Robinson's notes.

12 "Chaucer and Machaut's *Dit de la Fontaine Amoreuse*," *Vassar Medieval Studies*, ed. Christabel F. Fiske (New Haven, 1923), pp. 219-231.

13 Pp. 230-231.

NOTES FOR CHAPTER VII

1 The year 1333 also has some authority as Froissart's birth date. See F. S. Shears, *Froissart: Chronicler and Poet* (London, 1930), p. 224 (note to p. 2).

2 Ll. 2382 ff. of *Espinette amoreuse* seem to refer to this voyage.

3 Shears, p. 13.

4 Baron Kerwyn de Lettenhove, *Œuvres de Froissart*, I, Pt. 1 (Brussels, 1870); Shears, *op. cit.*; B. J. Whiting, "Froissart as Poet," *Mediaeval Studies*, VIII (1946), 189-216.

5 Chaucer's name appears in the *Chronicles* but once. See n. 27 below.

6 Whiting, p. 191.

7   Elle morut jone et jolie,

   Environ de vingt et deux ans;

   Gaie, lie, friche, esbatans,

   Douce, simple, d'umble samblance.   (ll. 246-249)

8   E cils à ce bel soleil d'or

   On l'appelle Melyador;

   Tangis et Camels de Camois

   Sont là ensus dedans ce bois.   *(Paradys d'Amours*, ll. 985-988)

9 George L. Kittredge, "Chaucer and Froissart," *Englische Studien*, XXVI (1899), 331.

10 *Oxford Caucer*, I, 462.

11 Particularly noted has been Froissart's enumeration of his works in the *Joli buisson de jonece*, written in 1373 (see note 24 below). Here *Paradys* is listed first. For a more complete discussion of this and other points which have indicated the precedence of *Paradys* over the *Duchess* see, among others, Henry Bradley, "Chaucer and Froissart," *Academy*, XLVII (Feb., 1895), 125-126.

12 "Chaucer and Froissart," pp. 321-336.

13 By how long the composition of the *Paradys* preceded that of the *Duchess* is problematical. Since it is dependent on Machaut's *Fonteinne amoreuse*, it cannot date from before 1361. One of the Froissart manuscripts says that his poems were composed between 1362 and

1394. See Julia Bastin, *Froissart; chroniqueur, romancier et poète* (Brussels, 1942), p. 17.

[14] I have checked the phrasal parallels between these two poems only in the case of the promise to Amant regarding his future protection by Esperance. In *Fortune* Esperance speaks; in *Paradys*, Amour:

Mais au partir tant te diray
Que, se tu as mestier de my,
Amie entiere, sans demy,
Me trouveras a toutes heures. (*Fortune*, 2818-21)

Fors tant je vœil et si ordonne
Qu'Esperance confort te donne
Et que tout dis te soit present
Quel grief que Desirs te presente. (*Paradys*, 1377-80)

Though there is little doubt of the derivation of the situation of *Paradys* from *Fortune*, the similarity in diction is not striking here. I believe that a more thorough comparison would reveal a like dependence of narrative and independence of diction in Froissart's poem.

[15] Scheler, I, 364-365.

[16] Froissart correctly identifies Iris as Juno's messenger at the beginning of the poem.

[17] Chaucer utilizes the central narrative of *Paradys* as well as that of the *Jugement dou Roy de Navarre* in his Prologue to the *Legend of Good Women*. See John L. Lowes, "The Prologue to the *Legend of Good Women* as Related to the French *Marguerite* Poems and the Filostrato," *PMLA*, XIX (1904), 641-658, for the relationship of *LGW* to *Paradys*.

[18] Lines of the *Duchess* (all in the frame story) for which the *Paradys* provides a source are 1-15, 23, 45, 222-223, 242-269, 272-275, 1324-25, 1330-34. In addition the *Paradys* provides the unique source for the name Eclympasteyr, used in Chaucer's exemplum, l. 167.

[19] One of the assumptions of Sypherd's *Studies in the House of Fame*, for example, is that Chaucer's vision poems belong to a genre made up exclusively of dream poems. See pp. 1-6.

[20] In ancient theory the dream before midnight was thought to be hallucinatory, but this idea did not control the conception of the classical poets and did not consistently affect the conceptions of medieval poets. See John B. Stearns, *Studies in the Dream as a Technical Device in Latin Epic and Drama* (Lancaster Press, 1927). pp. 51 ff. This question is pertinent to the *Duchess* since the poet wakes up on the

stroke of twelve. Bertrand Bronson thinks he wakes up at twelve noon: "Concerning Houres Twelve," *MLN*, LXVII (1953), 515-521.

[21] Sypherd in *Studies*, p. 10; Severs in "The Sources of 'The Book of the Duchess,'" *Mediaeval Studies*, XXV (1963), 357. See discussion of *Espinette* as possible source of Chaucer's "book" in Chapter IV above.

[22] *L'Espinette amoreuse*, ed. Anthime Fourrier (Paris, 1963), pp. 30-32. If the *Espinette* was written "aux approches de 1370," as Fourrier argues, then we must suppose that such a detail as the poet's asking leave to return home is wholly fictional, since Froissart simply failed to return to England after assisting at Lionel of Clarence's wedding, Philippa having meanwhile died.

[23] *Poésies*, I, xxi.

[24] Froissart's list of his long narratives in the *Joli buisson de jonece* seems to be in chronological order:

Voirs est q'un livret fis jadis
Qu'on dist l'Amourous Paradys,
Et aussi celi de l'Orloge,
Où grant part de l'art d'amours loge;
Après, l'Espinette Amoureuse,
Qui n'est pas à l'oïr ireuse;
Et puis l'Amoureuse Prison,
Qu'en pluisours places bien prise on;
Rondeaus, balades, virelais,
Grant foison de dis et de lays...   (ll. 443-452)

[25] Whiting, p. 201. An article concerning the occasion of *Bleu chevalier* came to my attention too late to discuss it in the text: Normand Cartier, "Le Bleu Chevalier," *Romania*, LXXXVII (1966), 289-314. In any event, I believe that Mr. Cartier's hypothesis that the poem was written in the 1360's for Louis of Anjou (who was a hostage in England along with the Duke of Berry), based as it is on a series of suppositions, is not likely. Consideration of the whole group of complaint-and-comfort poems, I argue, points to composition after the *Book of the Duchess*.

[26] For an example of Chaucer's practice in this regard, notice how his list of nonpareils in *Duchess* (ll. 1056-65) overlaps with the lists of Machaut in *Remede de Fortune* (ll. 107-127) and *Behaingne* (ll. 420-425). Note on the other hand how Froissart transforms Machaut's long exemplum of Seys and Alcyone in *Fonteinne amoreuse* into a short personal prayer to Morpheus in *Paradys d'Amours* (ll. 14-32) in which he introduces the name of Oleus and the even more unlikely Enclimpostair.

[27] The only time that Froissart refers to Geoffrey Chaucer in all his chronicles and poetry is when he places Chaucer's name beside that of Richard Stury in speaking of the ambassadors who negotiated the marriage of Richard II with a daughter of Charles VI. *Œuvres de Froissart*, ed. M. le baron Kervyn de Lettenhove, I, Pt. 1 (Brussels, 1870), 113-114. When Froissart returned to England in 1395, he again saw Stury. *Ibid.*, pp. 380-381.

NOTES FOR CHAPTER VIII

[1] J. Burke Severs, "The Sources of 'The Book of the Duchess'," *Mediaeval Studies*, XXV (1963), 361.

[2] Ed. Leopold Constans, *Romania*, XXXIII (1904), 490-539. See also the notice of C[harles-Victor] L[anglois] in *HLF*, XXXVI, 642-644.

[3] P. 499.

[4] *"Le Songe Vert:* Its Occasion of Writing and its Author," *Medium Aevum*, XIX (1950), 1-16.

[5] E. g., the fleur-de-lis would not be particularly suitable for Constance. Castile's emblem is a tower.

[6] *Mediaeval Studies*, XXV (1963), 355-362.

[7] W. O. Sypherd, "Le Songe Vert and Chaucer's Dream Poems," *MLN*, XXIV (1909), 46-47.

[8] *Songe vert*, ll. 174-198 and *Duchess*, ll. 583-594; *Sv*, 327-329 and *BD*, 673-675; *Sv*, 162-167, 326-353 and *BD*, 689-692, 714-742.

[9] P. 361.

[10] The Vulgate reads, "Et in diebus illis quaerent homines mortem, et non invenient eam; et desiderabunt mori, et fugiet mors ab eis."

[11] Arthur Piaget, *Oton de Grandson, sa vie et ses poésies* (Lausanne, 1941), contains almost all of the biographical information available about Granson and an edition of his extant poems. References to the works are to this edition.

[12] *Chaucer and the French Poet Graunson* (Baton Rouge, 1947), p. 27.

[13] Piaget, pp. 136-137.

[14] Braddy, p. 60.

[15] Miss Seaton summarizes *Love's Renewal* in her article on *Songe vert*, pp. 7-8.

[16] *The English Poems of Charles of Orleans*, ed. Richard Steele (EETS, London, 1941), pp. 156-178. For the relationship of *Love's Renewal* to the *Duchess* see notes to ll. 4746 and 4998-99. More extensive uses of the *Duchess* are made in some of the ballads which follow *Love's Renewal*.

[17] Ed. Auguste Scheler (Louvain, 1882). Jehan de la Mote also wrote a 4632-line *Voie d'Enfer et de Paradis*, and *Parfait du Paon* which has more than 3600 alexandrines. He was cited by his contemporary, Gilles de Muisis, for his "moult biaus dits." For additional information about this poet and his works, see Antoine Thomas, "Jean de le Mote, trouvère," *HLF*, XXXVI, 66-86.

[18] Rosenthal, "A Possible Source of Chaucer's *Book of the Duchess — Li Regret de Guillaume* by Jehan de la Mote," *MLN*, XLVIII (1933), 511-514.

[19] George L. Kittredge, *Chaucer and His Poetry* (Cambridge, Mass., 1915), p. 54.

NOTES TO EPILOGUE

[1] Demonstration of what the *dits* did *not* contribute to the *Duchess* is important to my article on the Marian imagery, "The Apotheosis of Blanche in the *Book of the Duchess*," *JEGP*, LXVI (1967), 26-44. I argue for Chaucer's originality in this feature of the poem by showing that personal descriptions in the previous *dits amoreux* contain little imagery associated with the Virgin.

INDEX

112, 115, 119, 124, 136, 140, 146, 149, 155, 173, 174, 176, 177; *Third Motet*, 135, 156; *Thirty-Eighth Balade Notée*, 73, 156; *Voir Dit*, 71, 74, 81, *82-85*, 102, 127, 129, 155, 171
Messe des oisiaus. See Jean de Condé
Muscatine, Charles, 2, 3

narrator in *dits amoreux*, 29, 67-68, 94, 97-102
Neilson, William, A., 3, 32, 39, 167, 169
Nicole de Margival, *Panthère d' Amours*, 19, 23 50, *57-61*, 125

Ovid, 8, 9, 47, 51, 52, 91, 116, 149
Ovide moralisé, 155

Panthère d'Amours. See Nicole de Margival
Paradys d'Amours. See Froissart
pastourelles, 98
Petrus de Riga, 149, 155
Philippa, Queen of England, 118, 119, 120, 129, 140, 147
Philippe de Remi, 167; *Conte d'Amours*, 167; *Jehan et Blonde*, 167; *Manekine*, 167; *Salu d' Amours*, 31, *36-39*, 42
Phyllis and Flora, 88-89
Piaget, Arthur, 144, 178
Prise amoreuse. See Jehan Acart de Hesdin
Prisons d'Amours. See Baudouin de Condé
prisons in *dits amoreux*, 34-35

Raimon Vidal. *See* Vidal
Regret Guillaume Comte de Hainault. See Jehan de la Mote

Remede de Fortune. See Machaut
Richard II, 119, 140, 177
Rickert, Edith, 85
Robertson, D. W., Jr., 12, 164, 166
Roman de la Rose. See Guillaume de Lorris *and* Jean de Meun
Romanz de la Poire. See Thibaut
Rosenthal, Constance L., 147, 148-149

Salu d'Amours. See Philippe de Remi
Scheler, Auguste, 127
Seaton, Ethel, 140
service of birds, 19-20
Severs, J. Burke, 127, 140, 141, 142
Shears, F. S., 119
Sir Gawain and the Green Knight, 46
Skeat, Walter W., 120
Songe vert, 107, 133, 134, 137, *138-143*, 146
Spenser, Edmund, *Daphnaïda*, 146
Statius, 149, 155
Stury, Richard, 133, 177
Sypherd, Wilbur O., 3, 61, 85, 127, 140

Thibaut, *Romanz de la Poire*, 19, 24, 26, *50-53*, 57, 106, 173
Thiébaux, Marcelle, 47
Tournois des dames. See Watriquet de Couvin
Treaty of Brétigny, 112, 118
trees in *dits amoreux*, 22-24

Vergil, 63, 88, 149, 155
Vidal, Raimon, *Chasse aux médisants*, 24, 39, *42-44*
visions in *dits amoreux*, 124-126
Voir Dit. See Machaut

REPRINTS FROM OUR COMPARATIVE LITERATURE
STUDIES

Through the University of North Carolina Press
Chapel Hill, North Carolina

2. Werner P. Friederich. DANTE'S FAME ABROAD, 1350-1850. The Influence of Dante Alighieri on the Poets and Scholars of Spain, France, England, Germany, Switzerland and the United States. Rome, 1950; Third Printing 1966. Pp. 584. Paper, $10.00.

10. Charles E. Passage. DOSTOEVSKI THE ADAPTER. A Study in Dostoevski's Use of the Tales of Hoffmann. 1954. Reprinted 1963. Pp. x, 205. Paper, $3.50. Cloth, $4.50.

11. Werner P. Friederich and David H. Malone. OUTLINE OF COMPARATIVE LITERATURE. From Dante Alighieri to Eugene O'Neill. 1954. Fourth Printing, 1967. Pp. 460. Paper, $6.50.

Through Russell and Russell, Inc.
Publishers, 156 Fifth Avenue
New York, New York 10010

1. Fernand Baldensperger and Werner P. Friederich. BIBLIOGRAPHY OF COMPARATIVE LITERATURE. 1950. Pp. 729. Cloth, $15.00.

6, 7, 9, 14, 16, 18, 21, 25 and 27. W. P. Friederich and H. Frenz (eds): YEARBOOKS OF COMPARATIVE AND GENERAL LITERATURE. Vols. I (1952) to IX (1960). Cloth, $6.50 per volume.

Through Johnson Reprint Corporation
111 Fifth Avenue
New York, New York 10003

3. R. C. Simonini, Jr. ITALIAN SCHOLARSHIP IN RENAISSANCE ENGLAND. Cloth, $12.50.

4. GOETHE'S SORROWS OF YOUNG WERTER, TRANSLATED BY GEORGE TICKNOR. Edited with Introduction and Critical Analysis by Frank G. Ryder. Cloth, $8.00.

5. Helmut A. Hatzfeld. A CRITICAL BIBLIOGRAPHY OF THE NEW STYLISTICS APPLIED TO THE ROMANCE LITERATURES, 1900-1952. Cloth, $12.00.

13. Horst Frenz and G. L. Anderson, eds. INDIANA UNIVERSITY CONFERENCE ON ORIENTAL-WESTERN LITERARY RELATIONS. Cloth, $15.00.

15. Dorothy B. Schlegel. SHAFTESBURY AND THE FRENCH DEISTS. Cloth, $12.50.

19. P. A. Shelley, A. O. Lewis Jr. and W. W. Betts Jr., eds. ANGLO-GERMAN AND AMERICAN-GERMAN CROSSCURRENTS, Volume One. Cloth, $15.00.

22. Harvey W. Hewett-Thayer. AMERICAN LITERATURE AS VIEWED IN GERMANY, 1818-1861. Cloth, $8.50.

23-24. Werner P. Friederich, ed. COMPARATIVE LITERATURE: PROCEEDINGS OF THE SECOND CONGRESS OF THE INTERNATIONAL COMPARATIVE LITERATURE ASSOCIATION, 2 vols. Cloth, $45.00.

26. DANTE'S LA VITA NUOVA, TRANSLATED BY RALPH WALDO EMERSON. Edited and annotated by J. Chesley Mathews. Cloth, $8.00.

28. Haskell M. Block, ed. THE TEACHING OF WORLD LITERATURE. Cloth, $6.00.

30. Oskar Seidlin. ESSAYS IN GERMAN AND COMPARATIVE LITERATURE. Cloth, $10.00.

34. William A. McQueen and Kiffin A. Rockwell. THE LATIN POETRY OF ANDREW MARVELL. Introduction, Original Text and Translation. Cloth, $8.50.

DATE DUE

OCT 16 79			
DEC 15 80			
NOV 28 1988			
DEC 20 1991			
GAYLORD			PRINTED IN U.S.A.